Problem Solving /
Decision Making

for Social and Academic Success

The Authors

Maurice J. Elias is Associate Professor of Psychology, Rutgers University, New Brunswick, New Jersey.

Steven E. Tobias is a psychologist in private practice in Somerset and Montclair, New Jersey.

Problem Solving /
Decision Making

for Social and Academic Success

nea **PROFEfIONAL LIBRARY**
National Education Association
Washington, D.C.

Printing History
First Printing: October 1990
Second Printing: April 1991

Note

The opinions expressed in this publication should not be construed as representing the policy or position of the National Education Association. Materials published by the NEA Professional Library are intended to be discussion documents for teachers who are concerned with specialized interests of the profession.

Library of Congress Cataloging-in-Publication Data

Elias, Maurice J.
    Problem solving/decision making for social and academic success
by Maurice J. Elias and Steven Tobias.
        p. cm   —. (Aspects of learning)
    Includes bibliographical references.
    ISBN 0–8106–3007–9
    1. Problem solving—Study and teaching (Elementary) 2. Decision making—Study and teaching (Elementary) 3. Social skills—Study and teaching (Elementary) 4. Social adjustment—Study and teaching (Elementary) 5. Academic achievement. I. Tobias, Steven.
II. National Education Association of the United States.
III. Title. IV. Series.
LB1062.5.E44   1990   90–34951
370.15'24—dc20   CIP

CONTENTS

ACKNOWLEDGMENTS

Our book has been informed by years of collaborative field research and development with teachers, administrators, and parents, most prominently through the Improving Social Awareness-Social Problem Solving Project of Rutgers University and the University of Medicine and Dentistry of New Jersey-Community Mental Health Center at Piscataway. We also are keenly aware of our many intellectual debts to thoughtful educators, child advocates, researchers, and others who share our deep concern with children and the education they receive to prepare them for both social and academic endeavors. These influences and individuals are too numerous to specify; let it be said that we are aware that this book reflects more on our role as compilers, synthesizers, and organizers than it does as inventors.

Consequently, we wish to give specific acknowledgment to the teachers and support staff at Benjamin Franklin Middle School in Ridgewood, New Jersey. It was there, appropriately, that our FIG TESPN model of social decision making and problem solving received its major school debut. The collaboration of Susan Faigle, Al Renna, Lorraine Glynn, and Roberta Muldoon was instrumental in breathing life into FIG and generating many refinements and improvements. Working with these educators was enjoyable and stimulating. We also wish to thank John Campion for first providing us with the opportunity to work in Ridgewood.

I (MJE) wish to express special thanks to the staff and students who work with the Improving Social Awareness-Social Problem Solving Project. Year after year, they bring special energy and fresh perspectives to working in the schools and never allow us to become complacent. The financial and collegial support of the William T. Grant Foundation and the Schumann Fund for New Jersey has meant a great deal to me personally and professionally because of the confidence they have shown in the work that is represented in this book and the continuity they have enabled me to maintain. Finally, I once again must marvel at the capacity of my wife, Ellen, and my daughters, Sara and Samara, to be understanding and helpful during the many months involved in working on a project and writing a manuscript. To them, I publicly promise to clean off the dining room table as soon as this book is actually in print. It is to them that I dedicate this book.

I (SET) dedicate this book to the women in my life. My wife, Carol, has had to make many sacrifices because of my absence due to work. She is equally responsible for my successes through her love, advice, and support. My daughter, Meg, for whom I work so hard, has a smile that makes me forget about how hard that work is at times. My mother, Ruth, has nurtured me in a sensitivity and compassion that led me to the field of psychology. And my sister, Susan, has been and will be my lifelong friend and confidante. They all have helped both to inspire and sustain me during my work on this project.

—Maurice J. Elias
Steven E. Tobias

PREFACE

There is a snowballing movement in the United States to provide students with the skills they need for the kind of clear thinking that leads to positive health behaviors, sound peer relationships, and the motivation to use school as a place of learning. These skills are the same as those needed to prevent substance abuse and other high-risk behaviors. It is important to look toward the adult world that students will enter and for which they ultimately will be responsible. We must prepare them to be able to respond thoughtfully in decision-making or problem-solving situations. While these situations occur now as they proceed through their social and academic routines, as the years proceed, students will face increasingly greater challenges.

The skills needed to competently handle these situations are referred to as *social decision-making and problem-solving skills*. They involve (a) a core set of thinking skills essential for successful decision making, such as the ability to understand signs of one's own and others' feelings, the ability to decide on one's goals, and the ability to think in terms of long-and short-term consequences both for oneself and others; (b) a set of "readiness" or learning-to-learn skills, which include the main areas of increasing self-control and building social skills for group participation and social awareness; and (c) explicit guidance in applying social decision-making skills in academic and interpersonal situations that occur throughout the school day.

Our point of view is that social decision-making and problem-solving skills are essential to sound growth and development. *Learning social decision making and problem solving is a developmental right of all children; systematic instruction in those skills—particularly beginning in the early grades—-is of equal relevance to children's future in a social world as is instruction in "traditional" academic skills.* When children have difficulties that lead to a need for treatment in psychiatric clinics, mental health centers, and adolescent treatment facilities, and the like, it usually is discovered that they have deficiencies in social decision-making and problem-solving skills. Treatment often consists of providing them with those skills. But not all children get the help they need when they need it. Resources are scarce and access is not always equitable. And why must trouble be the signal to provide a basic and necessary learning experience? The harsh price of "starting too late" does not require elaboration to those who work with children and families.

A related aspect of our point of view is the extent to which our instructional procedures and activities emphasize the application of skills and concepts learned in the classroom to a range of everyday academic and social contexts. This is a distinctive feature of the social decision-making and problem-solving approach when compared to other approaches in the social and affective, critical thinking, and prevention domains. We neither "hope" for transfer of learning, nor do we "expect" it. Rather, for the benefit of educators and other readers, our approach is structured to foster application of learning to "real life."

The program presented in this book differs from other social skills and related programs in another way. This book was written to serve as a practical in-service training program with specific techniques and activities that can be used by any school staff member, from part-time lunchroom aide to school principal, without a major commitment of time, training, resources, or support staff. We wrote the book in this way because we know the realities under which school personnel usually have to operate, i.e., with little available time, training, resources, or support staff.

"FIG TESPN" is the centralizing concept of the program. It is an acronym for a set of social decision-making and problem-solving steps that are essential for success in school, in the family, with friends, in the world of work, and in the exercise of the privileges and obligations of citizenship in a democracy. The steps themselves have much in common with those of other programs and many will be familiar to readers. We believe, however, that FIG TESPN is unique in that it provides continuity and consolidation of the process of learning and applying social decision making and problem solving. Learning is then solidified through application of the process to a wide range of academic and social areas.

WHERE HAS THIS APPROACH ACTUALLY WORKED?

This book has been informed by years of collaborative field research and development with teachers, administrators, and parents, most prominently through the Improving Social Awareness-Social Problem Solving (ISA-SPS) Project of Rutgers University and the University of

Medicine and Dentistry of New Jersey-Community Mental Health Center (UMDNJ-CMHC) at Piscataway. The ISA-SPS Project began in 1979 with local school district funds in Middlesex Borough, New Jersey, and has extended over time with research and development funds from the National Institute of Mental Health, the William T. Grant Foundation, the Schumann Fund for New Jersey, and service funds from county and state sources.

The ISA-SPS Project has conducted summer institutes and year-round staff development programs since 1983. Classroom-based materials have been found to satisfy elements of family life education and health education requirements, and have been designated by the New Jersey Department of Education as a model for substance abuse prevention in the elementary grades. The National Association of Private Schools for Exceptional Children (NAPSEC) has featured social decision making as a model program for special education. Materials for parents have received recognition by the American Psychological Association for Excellence in Psychology in the Media, and in 1988, the ISA-SPS Project received the Lela Rowland Prevention Award from the National Mental Health Association as the outstanding prevention program in the country. Finally, in 1989, the ISA-SPS elementary-level curriculum was approved by the Program Effectiveness Panel of the U.S. Department of Education's National Diffusion Network (NDN); it also received developer/demonstrator funding from the NDN for national dissemination as a federally validated program.

The approach is now supported by service delivery from the UMDNJ-CMHC at Piscataway's Social Decision Making and Problem Solving Unit and by continuing education provided through a joint Rutgers-UMDNJ Continuing Education Center for Social Competence Promotion, Social Decision Making, and Prevention. The base of the Project's continuing research and development activities is in New Jersey, where districts of all kinds—large and small, urban and rural, and communities of all socioeconomic levels—are working with social decision making. In addition, school personnel in New York, Massachusetts, Washington, Illinois, Ohio, Connecticut, Florida, Virginia, Pennsylvania, Michigan, Canada, and England have successfully carried out ISA-SPS programs.

Throughout the Project's research and development efforts, the active collaboration of school personnel at all levels has helped our approach to be relevant, realistic, enjoyable, and capable of fitting into a variety of niches in the educational routine. Most specifically, the FIG TESPN model presented in this book was developed for, and refined at, the Benjamin Franklin Middle School in Ridgewood, New Jersey, over a three-year period. To put it succinctly, our work is "teacher tested."

In the book, we have attempted to outline and give examples of a school-based approach to providing diverse student populations with a solid foundation of social decision-making and problem-solving skills at all grade levels. The techniques and activities discussed in the following pages are designed to become infused into the daily practice of teachers and the daily routines of all schools. Initially, some additional time must be devoted to implementing the activities. This should be viewed as an investment that will come to fruition in part through a more orderly and efficient classroom and more thoughtful learners. The larger benefits will take the form of increases in social competence, positive character, and achievement on the part of the students—hallmarks of better preparation of students for their responsibilities as citizens and leaders in a democracy.

—Maurice J. Elias
Steven E. Tobias

1. THE CENTRAL ROLE OF SOCIAL DECISION MAKING AND PROBLEM SOLVING IN EDUCATION

Decision making gives thinking a purpose. Through our decisions, which are based on what we have learned both in and out of school, we determine the course of our lives. We make decisions that affect both our success as workers and our success as people. Since this is the promise of education, it seems clear that the new paradigm should be: Schooling focused on decision making, the thinking skills that serve it, and the knowledge base that supports it. (73, p. 38)*

In the twenty-first century, students will be considered "educated" to the extent that they can make informed, responsible decisions to promote their own well-being and contribute to the well-being of others. In preparing the next generations for their roles as responsible adult citizens, educators and parents must strengthen children's ability to think clearly, carefully, and sensitively, particularly when under stress. This book focuses on specific techniques to help students become competent social decision makers and problem solvers.

We recognize that supporting students in becoming more thoughtful is a challenging task. Too often, constructive efforts to help students are overmatched by media shallowness, negative peer pressure, perceived attractive alternatives to hard work, household tensions and disruptions of all kinds, and a sense of uprootedness caused by social mobility. Lacking stable attachments to provide a sense of security and positive guidance, many young people find their values and goals influenced by media and peer portrayals of "the good life" and how to "make it to the top." Amidst these many competing pressures, teachers struggle to find a focus, a meaningful way to engage students in building the reasoning skills that research has shown are necessary for a healthy future.

---

*Numbers in parentheses appearing in the text refer to the Bibliography beginning on page 124.

The National Professional School Health Organizations have defined health as encompassing basic academic competencies, psychological and physical well-being, vocational competence, positive interpersonal skills and relationships, a sense of linkage with and responsibility to the community, and an orientation toward law-abiding behavior (57). The capacity to make informed decisions also has been delineated as a goal of comprehensive school health education and a necessary outcome of successful schooling (28). Importantly, decision-making approaches can be implemented in ways that do not overload the curriculum (44, 46, 48, 52). Doing so provides appropriate, systematic emphasis on what appears to be a core set of skills that underlie competent performance in many specific academic and interpersonal domains: social decision-making and problem-solving skills.

SOCIAL DECISION MAKING IS PERVASIVE

Consider how often children, parents, and educators are placed in situations that require them to make important choices. Choices begin when the alarm clock rings; they continue throughout the morning routine and accompany individuals during school, work, household tasks, and interactions with others. Consider some of the situations many students face each day that require thoughtful decision making:

- Should I work hard or not?
- Should I become involved in religion or not?
- Should I use drugs, alcohol, or smoke or not?
- Should I risk pregnancy or not?
- Should I vandalize or not?
- Should I drop out or not?
- Should I try suicide or not?
- Should I follow my friends' advice or not?
- Should I respect my parents or teachers or not?

Children's path into adulthood in a democratic society is bound to their ability to exercise critical judgment and make decisions, regardless of their innate ability, environmental opportunity, background circumstance, or cultural heritage. Their decisions reflect their personal identity and, collectively, shape our national character. Will they be oriented to contribute or to consume? To create or to accept? To care or to stand by? To lead responsibly or to follow uncritically? Even the simpler everyday

14

decisions—what to wear, where to sit, what to eat—are linked to the more critical decisions mentioned above by a common set of skills that influence the choices each person makes.

The central role of social decision making in education, then, has both an intellectual and an interpersonal basis. The former stems from recent work suggesting that children (and adults) are most likely to show the extent of their abilities in contexts that they value (63). For most children—particularly those traditionally seen as "at risk"—social activities are an important part of their lives; therefore, instruction in social decision making is likely to engage their abilities and serve as a force for specific and general cognitive, affective, and social growth. Rather than building on areas of weakness or disinterest, social decision making focuses on areas of potential strength and high salience (e.g., even for a school-phobic or shy child, social situations are highly important). This, in turn, facilitates children's continued engagement with school. The interpersonal basis is summarized well by London:

> The job of the schools is to make children competent intellectually...and decent interpersonally...They [children] probably cannot achieve these ends without a sense of altruism or achievement or integrity or self-control or self-esteem. They certainly cannot succeed if they are drunk, drugged, depressed, or anxious, if they are parents before they can be breadwinners; or if they must abandon school to escape brutality, neglect, or despair at home. (52, pp. 670–71)

EIGHT PRIMARY SKILL AREAS

While many skills are clearly necessary for social decision making, our research and development team has synthesized eight primary skill areas from traditions in education, psychology, and philosophy. These eight areas are presented in Table 1–1. (Also included is an instructional version of these areas, heuristically labeled "FIG TESPN"; this version is discussed further in Chapter 4.) Research has shown that deficiencies in these skill areas are a common denominator among children and adolescents who experience a variety of problems, including academic failure and dropout, substance abuse, antisocial behavior, teenage pregnancy, and social rejection (3, 6, 7, 33, 35, 36, 45, 46). To highlight the salience of these skill areas for effectiveness in school, peer, and home interactions, a description of each area with its corresponding instructional step follows.

15

Table 1–1
A Social Decision-Making and Problem-Solving Strategy: 8 Skill Areas

When children and adults are using their social decision-making skills, they are—
1. Noticing signs of feelings.
2. Identifying issues or problems.
3. Determining and selecting goals.
4. Generating alternative solutions.
5. Envisioning possible consequences.
6. Selecting their best solution.
7. Planning and making a final check for obstacles.
8. Noticing what happened and using the information for future decision making and problem solving.

An instructional version of the social decision-making and problem-solving skills, given the acronym "FIG TESPN" is as follows:

1. *Feelings* are your cue to problem solve.
2. *Identify* the issue.
3. *Guide* yourself with a goal.
4. *Think* of many possible things to do.
5. *Envision* end results for each option.
6. *Select* your best solution.
7. *Plan* the procedure and anticipate roadblocks.
8. *Notice* what happened and remember it for next time.

1. Noticing signs of feelings/Feelings are your cue to problem solve.

There are two aspects of this skill: signs of different feelings in *oneself,* and signs in *others.* When children have decisions to make, problems to solve, or otherwise feel under stress, their first reaction is likely to be *emotional,* rather than intellectual. This is especially true of those below high school age. They may try to beguile adults with their sophisticated language and cerebral airs, but adults should not be taken in. Remember your own years before (or even during) high school. Emotions are at the forefront.

Sometimes students are confused by their emotions. This can lead to panic, a fight-or-flight reaction, or giving up on what they were trying to accomplish. Therefore, students (and adults) are taught their Feelings Fingerprints (31)—the unique way in which their bodies signal them that they are in distress. For some, the signal is sweaty palms; for others, a stomachache; many experience headaches of various kinds; some have backaches, rashes, stiff necks, dry mouths—the list can go on. By

16

teaching students their Feelings Fingerprints and labeling the finger-prints publicly, teachers can help them to differentiate difficult, unarticulated feelings. This enables students to express feelings in words and serves as a "cue" for them to use their other decision-making skills.

Feelings of others also serve as a powerful cue that one might have a problem to think about. To the extent that students do not attend to signs of feelings in others, misinterpret them, or have a limited perspective for understanding them, however, they may reach decisions and take actions based on faulty premises. For example, young children tend to see the world in terms of sad, mad, and glad. As they grow, their perspective on the world extends to other feelings, such as pride, worry, calmness, and disappointment. But children with emotional distur-bances are less likely to show progress in their ability to look for and label signs of feelings. To become effective social decision makers, it is necessary for them to expand their feelings vocabularies (31).

A critical situation that affects many children is being left out of groups to which they want to belong. Either they are not asked to join the group or they have been rejected. Perhaps they have developed a reputation so that nobody ever asks them to join in. Interestingly, adults first learn about the problem through signs of different feelings expressed by the student. Think about a student you know who has been left out. Think about a time when you have been left out. What kinds of feelings have you experienced? Sadness, hurt, anger, frustration, confusion, and embarrassment come to mind; it is painful to stand on the side by yourself, with everybody knowing it. By teaching students their Feelings Fingerprints and labels for a range of feelings, teachers give them ways to notice and describe what they are experiencing. Then, rather than reacting with fight, flight, or just standing there and being overwhelmed by their feelings, they can learn to take constructive action.

Teachers can focus students on their feelings by asking, "How are you feeling now? How did you feel when you went to the members of the group and they said no (or when you learned you were left out)? How were the others in the group feeling? What did you see or hear that helped you know how they were feeling?"

2. Identifying issues or problems/Identify the issue.

Stressful or upset or uncomfortable feelings are usually a sign that an individual has a decision to make or a problem to resolve. By helping students move from their stress to identifying the issue or problem, we

17

enable them to use their thinking skills. We encourage them to put the problem into words: "Tell yourself what the problem is. When else have you felt this way? What was happening? Try to say, I feel —— because ——; or When —— happens, I feel ——." These questions give a focus to feelings and decision-making efforts and also serve to identify "trigger" situations that have led to similar feelings in the past.

Taking the example of the rejected student, we might learn that the student is feeling anger and frustration and ask her/him to put the problem into words. How might you put this child's problem into words? "I feel angry because I would like to be part of the group, but I can't." "When they say no to me and act mean to me, I feel frustrated."

3. Determining and selecting goals/Guide yourself with a goal.

Deciding on a goal is a necessary step in decision making and problem solving of any kind. Would people drive a car without knowing their destination? How much do participants enjoy or benefit from meetings when the purposes are vague? Can you not tell the difference between a school—or a classroom—with clear goals and one without them? Students growing up in families with little supervision, conflicting supervision from divorced parents, or mixed priorities between home and school inevitably feel stress because of unclear goals. This may lead to inactivity, incomplete activity along a number of fronts, or misdirected activity.

Peer pressure can be related to not knowing one's goals. Smoking among middle school students offers a clear example. Students usually smoke because they think that their peers do and their peers will be pleased if they also smoke. But students often overestimate the number of their classmates who smoke and, when asked about smoking in one-on-one discussions, they acknowledge that smoking is not their goal.

We help students focus on their goals by reversing the problem statements they make and asking, "What do you want to happen? How do you want things to end up?" We encourage them to visualize (picture, imagine, draw in their minds, describe in words, envision) what they would like to have happen, and to reflect on how their actions will or will not help them reach their goals.

4. Generating alternative solutions/Think of many possible things to do.

This is a familiar concept, often referred to as "brainstorming," or the nonevaluative generation of as many solutions or options or choices as possible. When teachers think of their students, from preschool through high school, they realize that some are more flexible than others in a number of areas, including creative writing, overcoming roadblocks in math, doing experiments, and relating to peers and authority figures. Flexible thinking is a learned skill. It begins by creating an attitude that encourages students to think that in most cases there is more than one reasonable way to solve a problem, cope with a difficulty, or reach a goal. By thinking of different options before acting, students are more likely to come up with better ideas, less likely to act impulsively, and unlikely to be passive or stuck when faced with a problem or decision.

We encourage brainstorming when we ask students to *think of all the things that might happen next*, whether in response to a book the class is reading, a newspaper article or current events story, a discipline problem the whole class is having, or their options after high school.

5. Envisioning possible consequences/Envision end results for each option.

Ask several students, "When I ask you to *think* about something you are going to do, what do you do?" Ask others, "When I ask you to *think* about what might happen before you do it, what do you do?" Finally, ask yourself what you do when you *think* about the consequences of something you might do. There is a tendency to ask students to "think" about consequences, but developmental research suggests it would be more effective to ask them to *envision* what might happen next because doing so stimulates and capitalizes on their representational skills (18). In our work, especially around application of social decision making to health promotion and substance abuse prevention, we find that visualization is the language of thinking about consequences. Students can more easily "think" about short- and long-term consequences, for themselves and others, and alternative consequences, if we ask them to picture, imagine, describe, walk us through, or make a mental video of what might happen. Having a picture in mind to carry around helps extend consequential thinking and makes it more likely that when children are away from kindly adult influences, they will keep realistic, sensible outcomes of their actions in mind.

6. Selecting their best solution/Select your best solution.

This deceptively simple skill has several key components. Phrased in this way, it emphasizes that the individual takes *responsibility* for actively selecting what to do (or not to do). It also clarifies that the reference point for selecting an action is the individual's goal, as well as avoiding harm to self or others. We encourage this skill by asking, "Which of these ideas do you think will help you reach your goal (without harming you or anyone else)?"

7. Planning and making a final check for obstacles/Plan the procedure and anticipate roadblocks.

Planning skills are being viewed more and more as among the key factors that protect children from harm due to difficult life circumstances (65). These skills refer to the who, what, when, where, how, with whom, and to whom considerations that are a part of making one's good ideas work. Indeed, most people can think of many talented friends, colleagues, and relatives whose good ideas run aground for lack of thinking through and following through on the detailed steps necessary to ensure that things happen as they should. There are reasons why teachers have *plan* books and use lesson *plans*, and why special education is organized around IEPs and instructional guides. The same reasons apply to everyday social decision making and problem solving.

Because lessons do not always go as planned, we emphasize the idea of *making a final check for obstacles.* Put simply, "What could happen so that your plan might not work out?" Good planners *anticipate roadblocks.* They look ahead before they start and use this knowledge to bolster their plans, or perhaps just to be more ready to deal with resistance. Envision the students you work with. You will see that some handle frustration better than others; some always have that extra pen or pencil, or extra paper. Some are very set in their ways; when things do not work out as planned, they seem to fall apart. These are examples of students who vary in a learned skill area—the ability to plan and to anticipate and plan for obstacles.

Teachers can encourage skill development in students by asking them, first, many who-, what-, when-type questions, once they have selected their best solutions, to help them develop a more detailed image of what they will need to do. Sometimes, at this stage of social decision making, it becomes clear that the best solution is not feasible. If this seems true, it is time to go back to earlier steps, review other alternatives, and perhaps even reconsider the goal.

Once a student seems to have a plan, ask, "What might happen to keep your plan from working?" If you think there is an obstacle that students are overlooking, you might say, "What if you go up to Ms.

Hriczko and she seems very, very busy?" or "What if you ask Mrs. Brailove and she says she really can't talk to you right now?" It is the responsibility of adults to help students learn that the environment will not always be receptive to them—even if they have done an excellent job of social decision making.

In our work with at-risk and special education students, we have been reminded over and over again of the fragile nature of their sense of trust and security. When they finally agree to work with teachers, to work on social decision making, to think through problems and choices and practice their plans, they are hurt tremendously when they try their best and the world rebuffs them. We have found, however, that by anticipating obstacles and roadblocks with them (e.g., "What if Mr. Stroop is having a bad day and won't respond nicely to you or even see you?"), they can be fortified by *knowing they did their best*, that their work and planning was not for nothing, and they can still have trust and confidence in the adults who taught them social decision making—as well as in themselves. (We have also learned much about the difficulty special education and at-risk students encounter when trying to change and improve because of the interplay of their own negative expectancies and the fact that a human environment offers many chances for rebuffs. The focus on obstacles has been a potent antidote to negativity and a valuable aid to positive motivation and self-confidence.)

8. Noticing what happened and using the information for future decision making and problem solving/Notice what happened and remember it for next time.

Think of recent conferences you have had with parents. Perhaps you have heard yourself or the parents say something like, "Jackie does the same things over and over again. It never works out. Doesn't Jackie ever learn?" or "Carmen repeats the same mistakes all the time. Doesn't Carmen remember what happened the other times?" The answer to these questions is often no. These children lack the *skill* of using the past to inform the future. They do not know how to recall their past experiences and see how those experiences can apply to what is happening now or to what might happen next. Jackie and Carmen may be kindergartners, sixth graders, or high school juniors. If they are to function well in the adult world, they need help with this skill.

When students learn to "try it and rethink it," they are learning that decision making and problem solving are *processes*. Our message is basic, but important in a world of instant gratification: "Go try it. Then, let's talk about what happened. Let's see what we can learn from it. If it doesn't work quite right, let's take a closer look at what happened and figure out what to do next." We hope to spark a spirit of experimentation, a willingness to work toward a desired goal, to think about the past and use it in the future, and to inspire self-confidence— "YOU CAN DO IT!"

Reading about these skills has no doubt triggered many images and associations. Perhaps you see yourself carrying out some of these ideas already. Perhaps you see how relevant they are to your personal decision making and problem solving and how the process of social decision making can be useful to you personally and professionally (cf. "Decision Making for Me" [17]). Most likely, you have questions about how these steps are put into practice in the schools. While the remainder of this book focuses on specific examples, some of the basic questions most often asked about social decision making are addressed next.

QUESTIONS AND ANSWERS

Aren't These Steps Hard for Students to Learn?

The use of an eight-step social decision-making approach represents a way to consolidate many broad and inclusive skill areas. It also represents our view that students need a social decision-making *strategy* they can apply in many situations. Realistically, we cannot prepare students for each and every problem and decision and all the ways in which they might occur. The *strategy* provides *continuity* over time, across experiences with different adults and in different places; it also provides *clarity* amidst the many competing influences on the student's mind. We see the eight-step social decision-making strategy serving as a beacon in a fog or as a lifeline for one who is overboard at sea. Indeed, the students who develop a coping strategy are those who are most effective in meeting school, home, and peer demands and responsibilities. With the unrelenting numbers of psychological casualties among students (10, 52), it becomes clear that whatever processes worked in the past to help prepare students for the roles and responsibilities of adulthood are no longer working adequately. *The eight steps become an explicit, clarifying strategy accessible to all students, not only to those who are skillful enough to extract a useful strategy from the complex and fast-moving world around them.*

The eight steps are no more difficult to learn than any other complex set of skills. Remember how you learned to drive a car, to do long division, or to read a map. At first, you followed a step-by-step procedure: "First, you put on your seat belt. Then, you check your rearview mirror. Next, ..." With time and practice, complex sets of steps and skills become "routinized" or "automatized" or incorporated into "scripts" or "knowledge networks" (4, 9, 60, 72). With experience, the same basic sets of skills are used, but they become broadened, extended, and further integrated. We never lose sight of the fact that the goal is to build the skills gradually so that students possess them when they are ready to emerge into the adult world.

There is no expectation that they can be learned, retained, and generalized without a degree of continuing instruction and infusion into academic content and classroom routines. As social decision making is taught, however, students quickly begin to realize the power and usefulness of *thinking*. They come to believe that they can be decision makers and problem solvers. They begin to feel a sense of "I Can" that they can build upon even while they are learning their skills. Through a combination of *confidence and competence*—the sense of "I Can" and the effectiveness of the skills in social decision making and problem solving—we have found we can fortify students against stressors and prepare them for the challenges of their teenage and adult years (27). Table 1–2 contains the comments of diverse educators on the relevance of social decision making to their work.

How Is Social Decision Making Relevant to At-Risk Students?

We believe that by teaching at-risk children to think carefully and independently through decisions and problems, we will help them see that they have choices, that they have some control over their lives. (55, pp. 138–39)

It is becoming recognized that the behavior of children who are at risk is characterized by impulsive decision making that appears to maximize danger and harm to self and others, as well as randomness (55). Yet, instruction in critical thinking and decision making typically is not emphasized for high-risk students (50). According to Mirman, Swartz, and Barell, "The extent to which at-risk students are afforded opportunities to engage in collaborative problem solving may determine whether or not they become less disaffected with the school" (55, p. 145).

Table 1–2
The Objectives and Relevance of Teaching
Social Decision Making To Children

Comments from Teachers and Administrators of Regular and Special Education Programs, School Psychologists, Special Education Aides, Substance Abuse Counselors, Learning Specialists, Social Workers, and Guidance Counselors

1. To become more successful participants in society.
2. To achieve greater success in school.
3. To give children the confidence to make positive choices.
4. To improve their quality of life by helping students make better decisions and assume greater responsibility in its direction.
5. To enable students to have greater self-esteem and a feeling of control over what happens to them.
6. To improve basic thinking that will affect all areas of their functioning.
7. To make children think through a problem before taking impulsive action.
8. To help children behave in a more socially acceptable way to gain peer acceptance.
9. To help children gain confidence and knowledge needed to make appropriate social decisions.
10. To consider consequences and alternatives.
11. To help children to set goals.
12. To better prepare children for full participation in the learning process, not just in the classroom but in all aspects of life.
13. To enable children to generate solutions to common everyday problems and help them become competent in social circles, situations, and interpersonal relationships.
14. To enhance students' abilities to interact socially in a more mature manner.
15. To give individuals an approach to handling problems that they can rely on across varying situations.
16. To give children more power over their lives, so they are better able to see cause and effect.
17. To enhance children's ability to deal with everyday problems in a positive, constructive manner.
18. To enhance interpersonal relationships.
19. To ensure future success in all the important areas of life—work, loving relationships, etc.

Engaging in problem solving and decision making of the kind described in this book provides at-risk students with a strategy that can correct the flaws in their decision-making process and highlight the relevance and benefits of mastering their feelings and pursuing goals in a focused, thoughtful way. Reducing risk status is a matter of increasing both the confidence and competence of students. A social decision-making and problem-solving approach provides skills and reflects an empowering attitude that students and educators can use to find elements of school that can be meaningful and engaging to students.

Can Social Decision Making Make a Difference?

> Decision makers play the roles of philosopher, scientist, designer, and builder. Schooling focused on decision making, the developmental and critical thinking skills that serve it, and the knowledge base that supports it, will allow students to learn these roles, to claim their capacity to think and their heritage as human beings. (73, p. 41)

Social decision making is not a panacea. It is an approach that can be of assistance at various levels. The eight steps have diagnostic value in helping educators uncover areas of strength and weakness. (Further discussion appears in Chapter 2.) Educators can also use the eight steps as part of a strategy to assist them in their own decision-making processes. With students, even on a short-term basis—during the course of one academic year with a class or a special group—there has been evidence of successful use of social decision making and related approaches (25, 45, 71). Finally, the best results appear to reflect the same features as for other academic areas: they occur when there is continuity over a period of years, reinforcement and application of skills at times other than during formal lessons, and support from school personnel at a variety of levels (31). We have seen the approach make a difference in a number of school contexts, but always in relation to the goals and scope defined by the educators involved.

Are All Students Ready to Learn the Social Decision-Making Steps?

In the initial years of the project, the ISA-SPS (Improving Social Awareness/Social Problem Solving) team followed conventional wisdom and began with instruction in the eight decision-making and problem-solving steps. This became known as the Instructional Phase, and was followed by a series of lessons and activities designed to foster application of the social decision-making process to everyday interpersonal and academic situations (the Application Phase) (31). As the ISA-SPS team began working with early elementary school-aged children, special education populations, and children at risk for poor adjustment, two sets of skills appeared to be prerequisites for effective social decision making.

Self-control skills are necessary if students are to effectively monitor interpersonal situations, accurately extract information, and remain involved in the situation long enough to begin to access and use their decision-making abilities. These include listening and remembering, following directions, calming oneself when under stress, and starting and maintaining a socially appropriate conversation.

Social awareness and group participation skills reflect the perspective that *groups of classes* learn and function best as problem-solving teams (70). Therefore, social decision-making instruction tends to occur in group situations, using cooperative learning methods (44). Key skills include asking for and receiving help, giving and receiving praise and criticism, selecting praiseworthy friends, showing caring, perspective taking, and sharing with the group. Lessons and activities covering these skill areas are part of the Readiness Phase, which typically is an initial target for work involving early elementary and high-risk populations (31). The inclusion of the Readiness Phase had led to increased effectiveness of the overall program and extended its scope to be relevant to more diverse groups of students. Indeed, in some districts, children focus mainly on self-control and social-awareness skills and do not emphasize the social decision-making steps.

The authors share a perspective summarized by Perry London:

> For the common good, a sane society needs to educate its citizens in both civic virtue and personal adjustment.... The schools must become more important agents of character development, whose responsibility goes beyond such matters as dress, grooming, and manners. Their new role must include training for civility and civic virtue, as well as a measure of damage control for personal maladjustment. (52, p. 67)

Social decision making skills can—and, we feel must—be built as part of the education of students in schools. Clearly, there also is much that parents can and must do (31). The urgency of a school-based effort is clear, however, as one considers the nature of school populations, the societal needs of an increasingly service-oriented and technological culture, and the role of the schools as the primary common, public socializer of children.

2. METHODS OF SOCIAL DECISION-MAKING INSTRUCTION

The questions we, as thinkers, can pose before, during, and after our engagement with problem solving are designed to affect our control over our thinking. . . . Why such a strategy would be effective with at-risk students should by now be obvious: by definition, they have little sense of competence within school; they are detached and unmotivated, and see little connection between their "real" lives and what goes on in school. Empowering all students with ways of planning their approach to a problem ("What is my problem? How will I solve it?"), monitoring their progress ("How well am I doing?"), and evaluating their success ("Have I finished? How well have I done?") should, ultimately, affect the conduct of their lives both in and out of school. (55, p. 146)

A number of very practical methods can be used to build social decision-making and problem-solving skills of students, as well as their self-control and group participation and social awareness skills. This chapter reviews the most common and effective instructional methods, focusing on those that can be easily integrated into the classroom routine. These methods include the use of prompts and cues, modeling, facilitative questioning, and television-based discussion and guided rehearsal and practice (TVDRP).

ASSESSING STUDENTS' SKILL LEVELS

The initial step in instructional planning is an assessment of students' skill levels. We have provided a checklist that educators can use to determine those situations in which their students display particular social decision-making and problem-solving skills. Clearly, one would expect younger students to display these skills across a narrower range of situations than would older students. It is important to note, however, that the checklist allows teachers to distinguish between competence and performance. That is, by knowing a student has demonstrated the skill in one situation, it is easier to work with him or her to build and use that skill in other, significant situations.

Table 2–1 is a checklist of the primary social decision-making and problem-solving skills identified through theory, research, and educational practice. Think of two or three students you work with, perhaps at different grade levels, with appropriate, not outstanding, academic performance and social relationships. Perhaps they are students you would view as positive role models. Ask yourself about the range of situations in which these students show self-control skills (A. 1–5). Think about the extent to which these students show social awareness and group participation skills (B. 6–10). Finally, consider the set of social decision-making and problem-solving skills (C. 11–29). It is likely that these students have exhibited many of these skills, particularly in school contexts.

Note that as you thought about students at different levels— elementary, middle school, high school—you probably found that the same sets of skills were applicable. This is because the skills are very basic to success in school and in the social world; as students mature, we expect more sophisticated application of the skills and increased complexity in their use.

Now think of several students who have difficulties with learning or behavior. Review their ability to use self-control, social awareness and group participation, and social decision-making skills in different situations. No doubt, you will find at least a few important instances in which their use of skills was deficient. In our experience, students with more severe problems tend to have significant deficits in self-control, and social awareness and group participation. These areas incorporate important prerequisite, or readiness, skills because (a) accurate information and perspectives gathered from these skills are necessary as a basis for effective social decision making and (b) difficulties in these areas transform situations and often lead to fight-or-flight reactions, rather than thoughtful reactions. Thus, we recommend that teachers recognize the necessity of addressing the readiness levels of their students and not focus on only social decision making or critical thinking skills.

As a final exercise, ask yourself how well a student would function with deficiencies in any one, two, three, or four of the skills on the checklist. Imagine if the deficiencies occurred in only two or three of the 10 situations listed. Is there any doubt that the student would be at risk for school failure and for lack of success as a healthy, productive adult citizen?

Table 2–1
A Checklist of Students' Social Decision-Making and Problem-Solving Strengths Across Situations

Student: _____   Date: _____

In what situations is this student able to use the following: Situations*

A. Self-Control Skills
1. Listen carefully and accurately _____
2. Remember and follow directions _____
3. Concentrate and follow through on tasks _____
4. Calm him/herself down _____
5. Carry on a conversation without upsetting or provoking others _____

B. Social Awareness and Group Participation Skills
6. Accept praise or approval _____
7. Choose praiseworthy and caring friends _____
8. Know when help is needed _____
9. Ask for help when needed _____
10. Work as part of a problem-solving team _____

C. Social Decision-Making and Problem-Solving Skills
11. Recognize signs of feelings in self _____
12. Recognize signs of feelings in others _____
13. Describe accurately a range of feelings _____
14. Put problems into words clearly _____
15. State realistic interpersonal goals _____
16. Think of several ways to solve a problem or reach a goal _____
17. Think of different types of solutions _____
18. Do (16) and (17) for different types of problems _____

_____

*Enter the number of those situations in which particular skills appear to be demonstrated, using the following codes:

1=with peers in classroom
2=with peers in other situations in school
3=with teachers
4=with other adults in school
5=with parent(s)
6=with siblings or other relatives
7=with peers outside school
8=when under academic stress or pressure
9=when under social or peer-related stress or pressure
10=when under family-related stress or pressure

29

Table 2–1 (Continued)

19. Differentiate short- *and* long-term conse-
    quences   _____
20. Look at effects of choices on self *and* others   _____
21. Keep positive *and* negative possibilities in
    mind   _____
22. Select solutions that can reach goals   _____
23. Make choices that do not harm self or others   _____
24. Consider details before carrying out a solution
    (who, when, where, with whom, etc.)   _____
25. Anticipate obstacles to plans   _____
26. Respond appropriately when plans are
    thwarted   _____
27. Try out his or her ideas   _____
28. Learn from experiences or from seeking out
    input from adults, friends   _____
29. Use previous experience to help "next time"   _____

INSTRUCTIONAL PROCEDURES

Table 2–2 outlines the techniques that tend to be most effective in facilitating social decision making and problem solving. This outline is set up in the form of a monitoring sheet that teachers or observers/supervisors can use to focus on teachers' skills in leading discussions designed to stimulate students' social decision-making processes. It contains four general categories: eliciting information, providing support, eliciting thoughtful social decision making and problem solving, and encouraging action. Eliciting information and providing support are genetic skills related to group work and discussion leading. The specific skills associated with eliciting thoughtful social decision making and encouraging action will be the focus of this discussion.

When attempting to teach students a new skill, it is important to break it down into clear component parts. To the extent to which the directions are clear about what students are expected to do, it is reasonable to expect students to learn the skill. The first thing they must learn, however, is to carry out the skill in a protected, practice situation. The next part of the learning process is not to carry over the skill to spontaneous use in everyday situations, but to be able to *use the skill when prompted.* Therefore, we use the technique of prompting and cuing to identify the component parts of a skill and to give the enactment of the components a clear label. This label, which serves as the prompt to use the skill and the cue to carry out the sequence of behaviors that have been taught, creates a common language that is shared among a group of students, as well as between educators and students (and potentially parents, educators, and students). This common language allows expectations for behavior to be clear and allows students' difficulties to be framed as a question of learning specific skills more proficiently.

An activity presented in Chapter 3—teaching students the self-control skill of calming themselves—is previewed and explicated here to show the seven-part prompt-and-cue framework.

A. Break the skill down into its component parts.
   Prepare students by telling them that today's activity will focus on ways of helping them keep calm when they are upset or when they face a difficult decision or problem. Next, tell them exactly what is meant by "keeping calm":
   1. Tell yourself, "Stop and take a look around."
   2. Tell yourself, "Keep calm."
   3. Take a deep breath through your nose while you count to five; hold it while you count to two; then breathe out through your mouth while you count to five.
   4. Repeat these steps until you feel calm.
      First, students are asked to stop and take a look around; second, they say to themselves, "Keep Calm," i.e., to access the prompt. The third part of Keep Calm is to cue the deep breathing and counting procedure, which may remind the reader of the Lamaze technique of relaxation. The next aspect is to continue the breathing until they feel calm.

B. Acquaint students with a prompt (or label) for cuing the use of the skill.
   The process of carrying out these four "steps" is given the prompt and label, "Keep Calm."
C. Identify opportunities in which students feel the skill would be useful to them.
   Ask students to identify situations in which they would like to Keep Calm. These are labeled as situations that "trigger" them to lose their cool, such as when they are rejected or teased by classmates.

Table 2–2
Techniques for Leading Social
Decision-Making Discussions

Please complete this section before any observing or taping and self-rating.

Name and Position of Leader/Facilitator:_____

Name and Position of Observer/Rater_____

Date of Observation/Rating:_____

Type of setting/topic of lesson (e.g., 23 fourth graders/review of Keep Calm):

_____

Used	Used often	
		1. Elicits Information
_____	_____	• attends to verbal and nonverbal messages
_____	_____	• reviews previous material
_____	_____	• uses the two-question rule (follows a question with a question
_____	_____	• allows wait time after asking questions
_____	_____	• clarifies comments and links to what others have said
		2. Provides Supportive Environment
_____	_____	• uses inviting, varied voice tone, clear, well-paced speech
_____	_____	• paraphrases students' responses and reflects feelings
_____	_____	• accepts responses and asks for others
_____	_____	• establishes clear rules (e.g., letting others speak without interrupting) and gives clear directions
_____	_____	• praises before criticizing; gives positive, constructive feedback
_____	_____	• praises, acknowledges participation
		3. Elicits Thoughtful Decision Making and Problem Solving
_____	_____	• uses prompts and cues (e.g., Keep Calm, FIG TESPN [see Chapter 4])
_____	_____	• models own thinking and decision making, own use of social decision-making steps

Table 2–2 (Continued)

_____	_____	• provides a balance of asking, suggesting, and telling; guides and encourages thinking rather than evaluating and providing "answers"
_____	_____	• uses facilitative questioning techniques (open-ended; how, when, what else, what if, what might)
_____	_____	• suggests use of self-control, social awareness, and social decision-making skills by students
_____	_____	• encourages covert rehearsal (visualization, drawing, writing)
_____	_____	• elicits linkages to students' personal experiences; starts with hypotheticals and moves to actual situations

4. Encourages Action

_____	_____	• elicits details of specific planning; makes linkages to what will be done in the future
_____	_____	• conducts behavioral rehearsal, guided practice
_____	_____	• uses TVDRP (see pp. 40, 43–46)

D. Identify opportunities in which adults feel the skill would be useful for students.

Teachers can suggest that it might be useful for students to keep calm before a test, when they are in an assembly program or a play, or when they are participating in sports.

E. Teach students the component parts through modeling the skill.

Teachers begin by modeling the Keep Calm steps several times.

F. Allow opportunities for practicing the skill.

Using the activities in Chapter 3, provide specific practice opportunities that allow teachers to observe students' use of the skills in the classroom and an opportunity for corrective feedback.

G. Encourage the use of the skill before situations in which the skill will be useful.

Once students have had an opportunity to practice Keep Calm, their next task is to be able to use this technique when prompted by the teacher. For example, before a test, the teacher might ask the class to use Keep Calm. Students would then take a few moments to look around, say "Keep Calm," practice their breathing, and continue until they began to feel calm. When the class comes back from a disruptive activity, such as gym or recess, the teacher might ask students to sit in their seats and use "Keep Calm" before beginning the next classroom activity. When students are upset after a fight, or perhaps after receiving an unexpected grade, the teacher can ask them to sit down and use Keep Calm until they are ready to talk about the situation. A variety of other opportunities for using Keep Calm with students will come to mind after referring to the checklist for social decision-making skills (Table 2–1).

Teachers often find it useful to set aside a few minutes weekly or biweekly and ask students who learn specific skills like Keep Calm to share times in which they have used the skill. These brief periods, which we have called "testimonials" (31), generate many ideas for the use of the skill that either would not be taken seriously if suggested by the teacher or would simply not have occurred to a student. For example, we have learned that a common situation in which students use Keep Calm is babysitting. Teachers would not typically recommend that students use this technique at such a time. In practice, however, once students have learned the skill and then feel stress while babysitting, they turn to something that will help them deal with feelings of stress and upset—Keep Calm.

Modeling

Modeling of decision making is particularly powerful. Students are not often exposed to the processes adults use to arrive at decisions and actions. Most typically, students see the outcomes of the processes. For example, students see classroom materials laid out for them when they arrive; they see assignments on the board; they see a series of projects that are due. Rarely, however, do they have access to the thinking and decision-making process teachers use to arrive at their instructional activities. In a similar way, students usually do not have access to the processes their parents use to arrive at their plans for the weekend; their choice of times to go shopping, of what to make for dinner or where to go for dinner; as well as a variety of other regularly occurring household decisions. The media makes unfortunate contributions to this situation. Because of their truncated nature, television programs—news programs, dramas, and situation comedies—provide children with inadequate insights into the time and detail required to think about problems and arrive at decisions.

For these and related reasons, it is especially important for educators to be willing to model aloud their own thinking for students. Naturally, to the extent that the eight social decision-making steps are a part of that thinking process, teachers would be modeling the specific steps that students ultimately will be asked to use. However, just modeling one's thought processes can be very powerful and liberating. This enables students to see that adults face consternation and uncertainty, and do indeed commit decision-making errors. By modeling their thinking and decision-making processes, in all their realism and with all their occasional irrationality, adults can empower students to think and to share their human, and therefore imperfect, thought processes. (See Table 2–3 for several examples.)

Table 2–3
Model Your Thought Processes: It's Worth The Risk

1. *The materials problem*:
   "I'll just go over to the cabinet and get out what we need . . . oh no! We're missing the glue and the poster board. Let's see . . . maybe we can manage without them . . . but I don't see how we'll get it to stick. Maybe we should just go on to some other work and I'll make sure I check the supplies next time before I do this. But you all look so disappointed . . . Maybe you have some ideas that I haven't thought of. How about some ideas? Tape? Perhaps . . . Double or triple the construction paper? That might work . . . Borrow from another teacher? Wow! This class can come up with some great ideas; I should ask you for your ideas more often. How about if we try. . . ."

2. *The equipment problem*:
   "This projector just stopped working. I'm not too good with these things. Let's try turning this knob. Oh, no! That ripped the film! So much for my mechanical skills. Let's get all the lights on . . ."

3. *The time problem* (the one that rarely happens):
   "Well, we finished the book with 10 minutes left. I really didn't plan to have time left over. What should we do? Maybe I'll have you get started on your homework. But that's not such a good idea, you won't get very far and you might rush. I know! Let's take out the assignments I just gave back to you. I can answer any questions about my comments, and I want to tell you about some areas you did especially well and some things we should probably review next week . . ."

Facilitative Questioning

A major technique for building social decision making is to ask students questions that encourage them to think. We refer to this process as facilitative questioning. There is an extensive literature documenting the educational importance of asking facilitative, or open-ended, questions (11, 37, 42, 76). For the purpose of simplification, we categorize the nature of adult-child conversations into three broad sets of options: tell, suggest, and ask. That is, when we speak to students, we may *tell* them what to do, with or without explanation; we may make *suggestions* of what they might do or think about; or we might *ask* them questions to elicit their opinions, using either a closed-ended or open-ended format. Table 2–4 gives examples of common academic situations and how they might be handled using these three options.

Table 2–4
Tell, Suggest, or Ask: The Consequences
of Teachers' Choices When Talking with Students

A student comes up to you during an independent work period and says, "I'm having a lot of trouble. I don't know what to do. How do I do this?"

As you read the range of typical, possible adult responses, pay particular attention to the cognitive processes required on the part of the student after each response. (The subject matter of the assignment is varied across responses to show the range of applicability of the points being made.)

Adult to Self (implicitly): I'll just tell Joe so he can get back to work.
Action: Tell, without explanation.
Example: "Just move the parentheses so that they come after the divisor and before the subtraction sign."

Adult to Self: I'll tell Elena and explain it one more time, in case she's not clear.
Action: Tell, with explanation.
Example: "Just draw the lines from here and where they meet is the location. Remember, find the starting points anywhere and follow the longitudinal line *down* and the latitude line *across* until they meet . . . that is the 'location'."

Adult to Self: Perhaps if I give Bill several ideas or choices, it will help put him on the right track.
Action: Suggest several possibilities.
Example: "You can take a look at the workbook and review the different parts of speech, or you might look over the examples we did last Tuesday, or you might try writing each sentence on a separate piece of paper and looking at them one at a time, instead of while they are together in the paragraph."

Adult to Self: I'll get Carol to think on her own and realize exactly what she needs to do.
Action: Ask a yes-no or closed-ended question.
Example: "Did you mix in warm water while stirring slowly?"

Adult to Self: I'd like to help Ron try to think this through on his own, to see if he really can grasp it.
Action: Ask an open-ended, facilitative question.
Example: "What are all the different things you have tried so far to figure this out?" or "How do you think Magellan and the other great explorers might have thought about this problem, and what kind of approaches would they try next?"

The literature is clear that the use of open-ended questions maximizes the opportunity for students to think and also maximizes their ownership of the resulting solutions or actions. By asking first, teachers do not limit their options to make suggestions to students if they do not know how to provide a useful response, or to tell them if they are unable to respond effectively to suggestions. However, analyses of questioning patterns in the classroom consistently show that there is a tendency to tell first, then suggest, and then ask (76). We are proposing that this balance be shifted so that asking is used more extensively.

To build social decision-making skills, a series of questions has been developed to stimulate the eight social decision-making steps. These questions and the steps they stimulate are listed in Table 2–5. When a student has a problem and receives a response through the use of facilitative questioning as presented in Table 2–5, she/he may be guided toward resolution of the problem in a way that encourages the feeling of a sense of ownership, responsibility, and investment. Further, this method shifts the role of the educator to facilitator rather than authority; the teacher now serves as a guide to effective thinking, rather than as a solution giver and problem solver. This helps to promote self-confidence, to build responsibility, and to enhance self-control, as students begin to realize that they can indeed be effective problem solvers and decision makers. In short, such questioning fosters a sense of "I Can."

In addition to the use of facilitative questioning, the kinds of techniques mentioned in Table 2–2 under Eliciting Information and Providing a Supportive Environment support the use of decision making in students. In essence, by using the techniques noted in the latter group, teachers create an environment in which students recognize that their thinking is genuinely valued and encouraged.

Table 2–5
Questions Teachers Can Ask to Help Students Engage in Thoughtful Social Decision Making

1. *Feelings are your cue to problem solve.* "How are you feeling? Am I right in thinking your voice sounds a bit nervous?" "You seem _____ . Where are you feeling _____?"

2. *Identify the issue.* "What would you say is the problem?" "I would like to know what happened, what's going on." (Encourage *specifics.*)

3. *Guide yourself with a goal.* "What do you want to have happen? What's your goal in doing that? How would you like to feel? What's your goal?" (Help make the goal clear and specific.)

4, *Think of many possible things to do.*
   "What are all the different ways you can think of to reach your goal? What else can you think about?"

5. *Envision end results for each option.* "If you _____, what might happen? What do you think might happen if you do that? What else? What might happen if you _____?"

6. *Select your best solution.* "Which of your ideas do you think is best for you? Which idea has the best chance of meeting your goal? Which one seems like the best thing to try?"

7. *Plan the procedure and anticipate roadblocks.* "What will have to happen so you can carry out your idea? What do you think could possibly go wrong or block your plan? How would you do it? When? With whom? To whom? What if things don't work out the way you think? What if_____ ? What else could you try?"

8. *Notice what happened and remember next time.* "What happened when you tried out your plan? What did you learn that might help you next time? OK, think about it and try it. We can talk about what happens, if you like."

Table 2–6 summarizes the perspectives of educators on facilitative questioning. Each educator has created a shorthand, practical, and personal version of the questions in Table 2–5 that can be used frequently.

When using facilitative questioning, teachers often find that students prefer to begin working with hypothetical problems or stories and gradually move to actual situations related to their own experience. These hypothetical stories are often abundantly available in literature that students can use for language arts. Table 2–7 provides a set of facilitative questions that can be used to analyze stories; it shows how each one can be linked to a social decision-making step. Such an analysis can be used with beginning readers as well as with middle school and high school students. Indeed, students who have learning difficulties often find that the explicit framework of facilitative questioning provides a helpful strategy for reading and understanding stories. The consistent use of this framework across different stories, even across different grade levels, synergistically reinforces both academic and social decision-making competencies.

Television-Based Discussion and Guided Rehearsal and Practice

Among the most powerful techniques for encouraging students to act is the use of TVDRP (24)—a combination of *te*le*vi*sion (or other audiovisual media), *d*iscussion (that will facilitate thoughtful social decision making), and guided *r*ehearsal and *p*ractice (or other forms of experiential activity). Considerable research shows that the use of television and related audiovisual media serve to mobilize students' attention, a key point if students are to become engaged in the instructional activities to follow (12, 25, 77). The combination of audiovisual activity, discussion, and rehearsal and practice or related experiential activity has been shown by Salomon (66) and others to have a synergistic effect on learning. Therefore, instructional procedures designed to incorporate the three TVDRP elements are likely to be more effective than procedures that use only one or two elements.

The instructional elements that characterize a TVDRP format are described in more detail in the following pages.

Television and Other Audiovisual Media

Well-prepared television material is a uniquely effective instructional

Table 2–6
Facilitative Questioning: Educators' Alternative
Definitions and Examples

1.a. *Definition:* Facilitative questioning helps students gain insight into their feelings and motivations. It gives them a handle or approach on how to deal with problems that arise in their lives. It helps individuals consider alternative behaviors that they can engage in.

   b. *Example:* A child cries because she doesn't want to go to school. First, question the child about her feelings. Then question about what happens in school. Find out how the child reacts in these situations. What specifically is making the child unhappy? Maybe the child is unhappy because of a misconception of the situation. Discuss possible solutions and alternative behaviors. Implement one or more solutions.

2.a. *Definition:* A way of helping students to utilize eight problem-solving steps by formulating questions to help them move through steps.

   b. *Example:* A child is left out of a group game. Ask Johnny, How are you feeling now? What is your problem? What do you want to happen? How could you achieve this goal? What could you do? What would be the consequences of each alternative? Which is the best solution to get the outcome you wish? Then, follow up. How did things work out for you?

3.a. *Definition:* A method of questioning that facilitates students' ability to recognize their feelings or feelings of others, placing a problem into words (objectives), questioning their goal, generating several solutions, planning a best solution and trying it.

   b. *Example:* A child "needs to get back" by yelling at a classmate in class who constantly teases her. The "yelling" gets the child detention on a repeated basis. The child could be given the opportunity to first recognize how she is feeling, how the teacher feels that she constantly disrupts the class, and how the other child feels when she yells out. I would help her recognize the problem—yelling out gets only detention, the teaser may stop by ignoring her. "Keep Calm" could be used to help the child become calm. I would have the child generate other solutions so she does not receive detention.

4.a. *Definition:* It is a way of helping individuals organize and clarify their thinking by different ways of framing questions that are open-ended or helping them probe their own thoughts. Not by being declarative or interrogative but more in a Socratic manner. It is a manner of keeping dialogue ongoing without making a judgment.

  b. *Example:* A boy wants to be mainstreamed but keeps fighting in class and has trouble understanding why he is not given the opportunity. I am thinking of a youngster who needed help in determining what were the differences between feelings and behavior. When I gave him some open-ended but specific "how"—and "choice"—kinds of questions, he was able to generate more thoughts, define the problem and goal and set up a plan to solve it.

5.a. *Definition:* The use of questions to raise the level of a person's thinking to a "higher plane."

  b. *Example:* It can be used to help students think through a problem they are having with their peers who are bothering them on the playground.

6.a. *Definition:* Aiding the student to define problems and to work toward developing solutions, rather than adults providing answers.

  b. *Example:* A child is being teased, is not skilled in sports, is the slowest reader in class, etc.

7.a. *Definition:* An eight-step process that helps children reason through a situation and come away with a better sense of themselves and their ability to cope with problems.

  b. *Example:* A child has been disruptive or has made a poor choice and then must accept the consequences.

8.a. *Definition:* A technique used to get the student to think about a particular problem or situation, to pinpoint the problem, to think of what the student wants to happen, the possibility of solutions and consequences, and come to a decision and plan.

  b. *Example:* Identify feelings ("Your face looks angry; it is red."); identify problem ("What happened?"); develop creative thinking ("What would you like to try?"); encourage confidence ("Those sound like good ideas"); teach consequences ("What would happen if you tried these?"); end with positive praise for thoughtful decision making.

tool. It can motivate students, direct their attention, provide relevant sample material, and be easily recalled. It provides an entry point for intra- and interpersonal learning experiences. Although parents and teachers lament the things children "pick up" from television and films, these media can be particularly effective with behaviorally and emotionally disturbed or disaffected, poorly motivated students. The principal advantages of television are that the quality of material tends to be higher than that of film (thus providing fewer distractions); it is a more public medium than film, as it can be viewed with lights on and others clearly present; and television or video materials will become increasingly accessible in the future.

Table 2-7

Facilitative Questions for Social Decision Making in Language Arts

Questioner	Skill Area Elicited
1. How did you feel about the story (book, essay, etc.)?	1. Identifying feelings
2. Who are the main characters and what are the main events of this story (book)? What problems, decisions, or conflicts did the main characters deal with?	2. Clarifying/identifying problem
3. (Select a focal character, event, or problem) How did _____ want the situation to turn out?	3. Selecting a goal
4. What are all the things the characters did to try to reach their goal?	4. Thinking of alternative actions
5. How did the different things work out?	5. Envisioning possible outcomes
6. What turned out to be the best solution? How did the characters finally decide what to do?	6. Selecting goal-directed solution
7. What if one or more of the story elements was different (character, setting, events)? What would have happened to the plan? What would have made it easier? Harder?	7. Planning and coping with obstacles
8. How is this story like other stories you have read? How is it like (title)? How would you change the story, if you had a chance to write it over again?	8. Using past and present experiences as a guide for the future

Discussions That Stimulate Problem-Solving Thinking

Whether one works with adults or children, an important goal is for participants to learn skills that they can apply across a variety of current and future situations. Social decision making and problem solving represent an important set of such skills. They include (a) the ability to calm oneself when upset; (b) knowing how to approach others appropriately in social situations; (c) understanding all participants' feelings and viewpoints in those situations; (d) being aware of any interpersonal problems and setting goals for resolving them; (e) considering a variety of alternative actions one can take, a variety of consequences to any action, and linking potential actions to consequences; (f) thinking through the steps one intends to take, including anticipating potential obstacles; and (g) monitoring the outcome of one's actions for future reference. Techniques for eliciting participants' social decision-making and problem-solving skills primarily involve the various prompting, modeling, and facilitative questioning techniques noted earlier (Tables 2–4, 2–5, and 2–6), and structuring discussions to gradually build these various skills.

Rehearsal and Practice

Across the entire domain of approaches to working with students, it is well recognized that direct interaction with them is the key to understanding them, and direct interaction among students is a potent learning tool. These methods result in teachers learning unique and important things about students and students learning to care for, respect, and become sensitive to each other.

TVDRP

TVDRP, then, reflects the synergistic effect of combining three instructional approaches. Additional evidence suggests that moving further into the experiential realm—through puppet play, skits, drawing, writing, storytelling, or other activities—consolidates gains from "TV" and "D" and increases the likelihood of generalizability and transfer.

Continuity

A successful program is likely to consistently reinforce and expand the skills it seeks to impart. Programs concerning social and emotional functioning often do not follow this educational principle. Rather, a single presentation might be scheduled, with little or no followup. TVDRP materials exist in abundance; activities can be planned around them at all grade levels. A common example is that of mainstreamed students. At the beginning of each school year, these students face the formidable task of gaining the acceptance of their peers. The use of video materials from Agency for Instructional Technology (1) series such as "Inside/Out" and "ThinkAbout" programs could be developed at the start of each year to help classrooms function more cohesively and supportively, and a climate of acceptance, understanding and appreciation of diversity could be established. Anticipating difficulties and working to prevent them from developing, rather than waiting until problems become severe before acting, is a potent way to smooth the mainstreaming process (34).

The general procedure for conducting an instructional unit based on TVDRP is as follows:

1. **Prepare** students for the lesson(s), often by discussing the relevance of the topic for them and by providing background reading.
2. **Review** how the lesson or activity connects with previous lessons.
3. **Orient** students on what you would like them to learn, and give examples.
4. **Focus** students on what you would like them to attend to particularly when watching the audiovisual presentation.
5. **Show** the audiovisual material.
6. **Discuss** the presentation by reviewing the sequence of action, using facilitative questioning to focus on the issues experienced by the characters, their use of particular social decision-making skills, and any links between their experiences and those of the students.
7. **Rehearse and practice** carrying out different decisions and problem solutions, emphasizing students' use of focal skills.
8. **Summarize** what has been covered at whatever stopping point is reached.
9. **Continue** the learning process through experiential activities that use the skills that students have learned.

This sequence typically extends over more than one lesson. However, it represents an effective instructional unit that has been of particular value in the context of teaching social decision making to students (31). Chapters 4 and 5 present examples of TVDRP in the context of particular goals.

SUMMARY

The instructional procedures discussed in this chapter have been used to build both social decision-making skills and students' general academic abilities. Chapters 3 and 4 contain extended examples drawn from curricula and lessons in use in the schools, showing how these procedures can be combined for classroom use across grades, over time, and with a variety of populations.

3. ACTIVITIES TO PROMOTE SELF-CONTROL, SOCIAL AWARENESS, AND GROUP PARTICIPATION

> Modern American society has lost much of its dependable common rituals, objects, and figures of reverence. . . . Nor are models of socially acceptable adult roles available as often or in as much variety as in the past. . . . It is not mere rhetoric to speak of the changed experience of these times as "social disorganization," nor is it fanciful to worry that these changes may have a troubling impact on character develop-ment. From the statistics that document social disorder, we may guess that the impact of these changes on individual character and, eventually, on the national character must be negative and may be severe. . . . The schools must become more important agents of character development, whose responsibility goes beyond such matters as dress, grooming, and manners. Their new role must include training for civility and civic virtue, as well as a measure of damage control for personal maladjustment. . . . (52, p. 670)

Before beginning to teach and use social decision-making and problem-solving skills, it is often helpful to build readiness by establishing certain self-control and social awareness group participation skills. (Of course, one can focus on these skills without seeing them as leading to decision-making instruction.) The teacher typically uses an interactive format in conducting the upcoming social decision-making lessons; therefore, greater control over classroom behavior is necessary. Students engage in group discussion and support one another in their problem-solving efforts; they need to have a feeling of belonging to the group and a willingness to share their experiences. In addition, they require self-control in the classroom and in other situations where social decision-making skills are used. They also need to be able to communicate effectively with others in an assertive rather than a passive or aggressive manner. The following activities and techniques are a means of introducing these skills to students; throughout, the teaching techniques discussed in Chapter 2, particularly prompting and cuing, should be used consistently. By so doing, teachers provide students with a strong start on a lifelong process of accomplishing the learning and everyday use of the skills.

KEEPING BEHAVIOR IN BOUNDS

Whenever students are engaged in lessons that are less didactic and formal than usual and in which they are encouraged to express their ideas openly, there is an increased opportunity to engage in inappropriate behavior. The teacher must walk a fine line providing structure and limits for students, while at the same time encouraging open expression and independent thinking. Successful social decision-making instruction requires students to learn to think for themselves in order to make successful life decisions.

In order to walk the line between limits and freedom, strong consideration should be given to the need for establishing a behavior management system for the classroom. The ideas to follow concerning behavior management are derived from principles of social learning and operant conditioning (15, 23, 38, 53, 59). The purpose of such a system is to give students feedback on their behavior in terms of what is appropriate and inappropriate, and to provide them with consequences that will motivate them to engage in appropriate behavior. The system should be administered in a matter-of-fact manner and be part of the general classroom routine. Expressions of anger by teachers and other adults during disciplinary encounters with students would be antithetical to the purpose of social decision making and would undermine the effective use of these techniques.

One simple technique that teachers have found to be effective for younger students is one minute of after-school detention for each instance of calling out or other inappropriate behavior. Students' names are put on the board or on a chart and each time they behave inappropriately, a slash mark is added next to their names. If they protest, another slash mark is added. It is important for the teacher to continue with whatever else is happening in the classroom while adding these marks. This avoids giving the inappropriate behavior a great deal of teacher attention and disrupting the general flow of the lesson. The teacher should explain this program to students before implementing it. Behaviors that will warrant a minute of after-school waiting time or detention should be delineated clearly to students in advance of deducting time for violations. (Of course, behaviors can be added or changed as needed.) When writing slash marks on the board, no explanation should be given. Discussion should occur either when the program is being set up, or after school before the detention time starts. In schools where detention is not a viable alternative, some other form of punishment should be used that is at least mildly aversive to students and is consistent with school policy.

The second technique found to be useful—"Three Strikes and You're Out"—is similar to the first but in a different form. For each instance of inappropriate behavior, the student is given a "strike." When the student has received three strikes, he or she is "out." An out earns a time-out in the back of the classroom, or some other mild negative consequence. After this, the student may continue to collect strikes and outs until he or she has received three outs during the period. At that time, a more severe consequence should be administered, such as being sent to the principal, formal detention after school, a note home to parents, etc. Again, it is important to define in advance the behaviors that will receive strikes, to administer strikes and outs calmly without disrupting the class, and to use these or related techniques systematically and consistently.

Behavior management systems that focus on the group rather than individuals also can be helpful. For example, the teacher can establish a baseline rate for inappropriate behavior, such as 10 instances of calling out, rude noises, and put-downs for each period. If students receive fewer than 10 instances, they earn a choice of activity, such as time at the computer, a learning game, or time in the school library. More than 10 can result in the loss of a privilege. An alternative could be to give 10 minutes toward a special activity each day that could be redeemed on Friday. Each time any student behaved inappropriately, one minute would be taken off. Whatever time was left each day could then be redeemed on Friday when the class could have a special activity or educational game. Teachers can and must be creative in the use of rewards and negative consequences. Keep in mind that rewards should be pleasurable to students and negative consequences should be aversive (i.e., some students dislike educational games and others thrive on the attention they receive in after-school detention). Also, systems need to be overhauled and sometimes radically changed periodically.

For older students, techniques involving individualized contracts may be most effective. A contract is an agreement between two or more people that delineates the responsibilities of each party. Simply stated, "If you do this, then I'll do that." The teacher may wish to introduce the concept of contracts to the class as a whole and generate discussion around the importance of contracts for society. The teacher can develop a contract for the class as a whole or for an individual student that explicitly states the responsibilities of the class and or student(s) (e.g., completing assignments within the specified time period, handing in homework daily, treating each other and the teacher with respect, talking at appropriate times in the classroom, refraining from aggressive behavior). A system for monitoring these responsibilities will be necessary; therefore it should not be so complex that the monitoring is inaccurate or inconsistent. Students can be made responsible for their own monitoring if there is some way of checking reliability. Of utmost importance is that the behaviors listed in the contract be clear, precise to all parties concerned, and relatively few in number.

The next phase of contract development requires negotiation and determination of the responsibilities of teachers and students. Although students probably "should" be doing the things outlined in the contract, at the present time they may not be motivated to do so. Some students often lack internal motivation to learn because of their frequent experiences with failure. Also, they may not be motivated to please others because of their conflicted social relationships. In these cases, it will be necessary to identify with each student what is motivating to her/him. The Premack Principle (61) may be useful here. According to this principle, activities that are engaged in voluntarily and frequently can be used to reinforce behaviors that are infrequently engaged in. For example, a student who spends free time in a vocational preparation class can be allowed extra time in that class if he or she has completed assignments in other classes.

It is important to negotiate the terms of the contract. A contract that is imposed on the student will not be successful. It is necessary, too, that the student feel a part of its development in order to buy into it. Usually, when students feel that the teacher is listening to them and is considerate of their needs, they will generate contracts with appropriate terms. Some students will make demands on themselves that go beyond those of the teacher. In such cases, make sure that the terms of the contract are obtainable.

Once the behaviors required of students, the contingent teacher behaviors, and the method of monitoring are delineated, it is necessary to draw up a formal, written contract that is signed by all concerned parties. This part of the process makes it more concrete, lets students know that the teacher will comply with the terms, and emphasizes the contract's importance. Time frames can also be included in the contract so that review and renegotiation occur on a regular basis.

ESTABLISHING A CLASSROOM CONSTITUTION

The next readiness skill area that requires consideration is the cohesiveness of the group. Feelings of trust and tolerance among students allow them to begin to share some of their experiences and to benefit from the experiences of others. The group behavior management program described above may be helpful, as students are given motivation to learn to help one another behave appropriately.

In a complementary way, a formal lesson involving establishment of a classroom constitution teaches students the importance of rules and gives them an experience of group decision making.

The objectives of the classroom constitution lesson are as follows:

- To engage students in a democratic and interactive rule-setting process.
- To discuss and develop social norms for classroom behavior.
- To establish a reference for reminding students of behavioral expectations and prompting appropriate social behavior.

The teacher first introduces the lesson by reviewing any past lessons on the United States Constitution or discussing it in a general manner. A review of the vocabulary and concepts related to the Constitution may also be helpful, such as constitution, article, amendment, law, contract, rights, and responsibilities.

Next, discuss with students why a constitution is important, i.e., what would happen if there were no constitution or law. Also discuss in what ways a constitution would be helpful to the class. (Some desirable responses include help maintain order, facilitate respect for one another, establish rules that both student and teacher would have to abide by, enable students to know what is expected of them.)

Generate a list of "articles" for appropriate classroom behavior. This list should be wide open and should encompass whatever students and teacher believe are important. Include both do's and don'ts. Write down all proposed articles in a brainstorming process and then review and edit them.

Review the final constitution with students and take a vote to adopt it. Indicate that this will now be the "law" of the classroom. Also indicate that the constitution can be amended if the need arises—in other words, if further clarification or additional rules are necessary. If students reject the constitution, explain to them that the alternative to a democracy is a dictatorship and that you, the teacher, will gladly serve as dictator if

51

they do not wish to exercise their democratic rights. Also inform students that you will act as a supreme court that holds the responsibility for interpreting the constitution.

Students can engage in several activities that expand upon the constitution. For example,

1. They can make copies of the constitution, using fancy lettering or a computer, if available. They can include an eagle or some other symbol to embellish the document.
2. They can make a classroom poster of the constitution. This can be a group project.

When developing the constitution, attempt to state rules in a positive manner. For example, instead of "Don't interrupt," the rule may be phrased, "Students have the right to speak and to be listened to by others." The initial generation of the rules should be without censorship or criticism. When editing them into a final version, try to get a consensus or agreement.

State rules as specifically and behaviorally as possible. For example, "Be nice to others" can be defined as not talking out of turn, asking permission to borrow something, etc. Specifics can be generated by asking, "What would 'nice' look like?" or "If you were being nice, what would or wouldn't you be doing?"

Subsequent to this lesson, when rules are violated, remind students of the constitution (sometimes just by pointing to it), that they generated the rules and agreed to abide by them. This can be done in a matter-of-fact manner, such as, "Article 5 of our constitution states that students will refer to other students by their proper names or commonly accepted nicknames (rather than as 'stupid' or 'jerk')." Continue to refer to the constitution throughout the year, revising it as necessary. If you have the same class over a period of several years, you can call a constitutional convention at the beginning of the year to review and revise the constitution as necessary.

USING SMALL GROUP INSTRUCTION

Other group-building exercises can involve the class as a whole on a project, requiring each person or subgroups of students to complete a part. Students can engage in peer teaching or peer tutoring activities, helping one another learn, and receiving grades based on how much each team has learned pre- to post-test. Several excellent references give details of how to implement these techniques (13, 14, 64, 68, 69). For example, groups of students can be assigned to be different countries. Each member of the group is assigned a different area of expertise to develop, such as history, economics, political system, art and culture, geography and transportation. Students either research their areas or receive materials from the teacher. They are then required to teach each other in their groups about their areas, after which the group as a whole makes a presentation to the class. Students could be tested on three levels: individual area, knowledge of the country, and knowledge of all the countries. This type of learning also has applications to drug education and family life curricula.

Another method of peer teaching is to divide the class into teams to master a certain amount of material. The teams can then compete in television game-show formats such as "Jeopardy" with each team member answering in turn. In order to win, the more advanced students have to help those less advanced. This strategy has been found to help all levels of students learn at a faster rate. Groups of students can be given problems to solve, social experiments to conduct, and/or class presentations that require cooperation and coordination among members. Grading can be based on a group's overall performance, as well as on the degree of cooperation and an equal division of responsibilities among group members.

BUILDING STUDENTS' SELF-CONTROL SKILLS

Perhaps the most difficult but most important instructional task is that of teaching self-control and proper communication skills. Students may have effective social decision-making and problem-solving skills and, in certain circumstances, be able to put them to positive use; without self-control and assertiveness, however, they may act impulsively or succumb to peer pressure. For example, even though students are taught the dangers of drugs and can verbalize worthwhile social values, they may not translate such learning into thoughtful behaviors when confronted with pressures from within or without.

The Keep Calm activity, derived from *Social Decision Making Skills: A Curriculum Guide for the Elementary Grades* (31), is designed to help students stop and think before acting. It is a means of reducing impulsivity and giving students a chance to separate their emotional reaction from their cognitive and behavioral reaction. This enables them to base their action on thoughtfulness, in addition to affective information.

The objectives of the Keep Calm lesson are to—

1. Point out problematic situations where students can use self-control to calm them down before reacting

2. Teach students, through a deep-breathing and stress-distracting exercise, how to become calm and maintain self-control in a problematic situation.

3. Practice a deep-breathing and stress-distracting exercise.

To begin the lesson, explain to students that, at one time or another, everyone encounters a conflict or problem situation that needs to be solved. This can be a problem in school or a problem with other students, teachers, parents, or friends. Sometimes people might jump right in and try to deal with the problem before they are ready. Today's lesson is to learn how to stay calm and keep self-control in a conflict situation in order to be ready to deal effectively with the problem.

Ask students what it means to use *self-control*. Ask them to tell about different *times* and *situations* in which they have to use self-control. Then, ask for ways they *show* self-control, or *things they do* to keep self-control. Write these examples on the board.

Explain that our bodies send us signals that we are about to lose our self-control. These signals of feeling upset are called *Feelings Fingerprints*. Some people get headaches, a nervous stomach, a stiff neck, or sweaty palms. Model for the class situations in which you felt upset and what your Feelings Fingerprints were. Have students generate examples of situations in which they felt upset and what their Feelings Fingerprints were. Label these *Trigger Situations*. List the Feelings Fingerprints on the board. Emphasize that Feelings Fingerprints are helpful because they warn us that we are in a tough situation and need to use self-control to keep calm.

Tell students that when someone bothers them, when they are having a difficult time, when they are in a *Trigger Situation,* or when they notice their *Feelings Fingerprints,* it is important to *Keep Calm* before trying to solve the problem.

Distribute the Keep Calm handout to the class (see Table 3–1) and ask students to read it. Also put up, or point out, a poster listing the steps. Keep Calm works to produce self-control in three stages:

1. Repetition of the Keep Calm steps aloud with the teacher prompting the use of each step individually.
2. Repetition of the Keep Calm steps to oneself in a whisper and using the entire procedure when prompted.
3. Silent and spontaneous repetition of Keep Calm by the student.

First, have the class read the Keep Calm steps aloud. Then, ask a student to lead the group in some physical activity that students can perform at their seats (jumping jacks, running in place, etc.). After one or two minutes of activity, say to students, "All right, let's use Keep Calm. Say "stop'...say 'keep calm'...take a deep breath through your nose while counting to five, hold it to a count of two, breathe out through your mouth to a count of five. How many of you are starting to feel calm?" (As necessary, repeat Keep Calm.)

For the second stage, use a similar physical activity, except start by saying, "When I say 'NOW,' use Keep Calm to calm yourselves down. Say the Keep Calm in a whisper. Look at the poster if you forget the steps."

At the third stage, when students return from lunch, recess, gym, or some other unsettling activity, ask them to use Keep Calm silently. Develop signals or cues for students to use to tell you when they are calm.

Table 3–1
KEEP CALM

Keep Calm is something that will help you get ready to solve problems and handle your trigger situations. There are four simple steps to remember.

1. Tell yourself, "STOP AND TAKE A LOOK AROUND."
2. Tell yourself, "KEEP CALM."
3. Take a deep breath through your nose while you count to five, hold it while you count to two, then breathe out through your mouth while you count to five.
4. Repeat these steps until you feel calm.

It is important to continue to prompt the use of Keep Calm when a student is upset, beginning to lose control; it can also be used before tests, school plays, or any other anxiety-provoking or trigger situation. (For older students, school dances, job interviews, and peer pressure to try dangerous or antisocial actions are times to use Keep Calm.) The following script may be helpful:

Say:

Use your Keep Calm steps.
Stop and think about what's happening.
Can you feel your Feelings Fingerprints?
Let's Keep Calm and calm ourselves down.
Let's take a look at what's going on. Tell me what happened, how you
  are feeling (etc.).
Take another deep breath and relax and then we can talk about it.

Keep Calm can be reinforced through several activities. Have students *keep a list of situations that are coming up or that they can anticipate* where using Keep Calm will be helpful to them. Also have them *keep track of situations when they should have used Keep Calm.* And present examples to rehearse and practice preparing for difficult situations or getting upset using Keep Calm.

Some students, especially older ones, may balk at using Keep Calm. For these students, it can be helpful to introduce this strategy as one very similar to exercises developed by sports psychologists and managers of musicians of all kinds to enhance athletic and musical performance. Discuss anxiety-provoking situations (asking for a date, going for a job interview) and how anxiety interferes with performance. Ask students to watch athletes (baseball batters and olympic divers give especially good demonstrations) before performing a feat that requires concentration and skill in the face of stress. Have the students notice that the athletes take a breath or engage in a self-calming activity. This is exactly what Keep Calm is. (An example of musicians can be used instead of or in addition to that of athletes.) Then, try to have students correct these points in their own social and academic "performances."

Another technique that fosters self-control and the inhibition of impulsivity is the use of *self-verbalization.* For example, when having difficulty with an activity, people tend to talk themselves through it. The teacher can model this technique for students numerous times during the day whenever it is necessary to make a decision. As mentioned in Chapter

2, it is beneficial to let students in on adult thought processes, from which they can learn much. Also encourage students to verbalize what they are thinking. Enlist students in sharing times they or their friends "talked themselves through" some problem or decision. The use of the facilitative questioning method described in Chapter 2 may be necessary to encourage students to do this. The process of this kind of dialogue, however, can result in a strong individual and classroom sense of "I Can."

IMPROVING INTERPERSONAL COMMUNICATION SKILLS

In addition to external controls (behavior management, group cohesion) and internal controls (keep calm, self-verbalization), it is also necessary for students to assert themselves and exercise appropriate controls on their environment through effective communication. Lessons in everyday communication procedures can—

- Teach students to distinguish between passive, aggressive, and confident styles of behavior.
- Teach students to distinguish between passive, aggressive, and confident styles in the following four components of behavior:
  B—**B**ody posture
  E—**E**ye contact
  S—Things to **s**ay
  T—**T**one of voice[1]

Explain to students that they will be learning how to be their "BEST" in difficult situations. "BEST" refers to a way of communicating with others that enables communicators to be sure of themselves and to increase their chances of being understood and respected by others.

Further explain that there are three different ways to communicate with another person: the Blaster (aggressive), the Shrinker (passive), or the Me (effective). Aggressive, pushy, and bossy toward others, Blasters do not care about other people's feelings and try to get what they want

---

Adapted from Elias and Clabby's VENT acronym and lesson activity (31), with the assistance of Linda Bruene. VENT refers to **V**oice tone, **E**ye contact, **N**ice language (no cursing), and **T**all posture. While this technique has been used effectively with students of all age levels, young children and special education populations through early adolescence tend to prefer BEST.

by bullying others. They do not consider other factors and other people in trying to achieve their goals. Ask students what might happen if Blasters try to get what they want in an aggressive way. Try to elicit the response that although they may sometimes get what they want, others will not like them and this may interfere with their ability to get what they want in the long run.

Meek and passive, Shrinkers seem to care more about what others want than what they want. Shrinkers do not stand up for themselves or try to get what they want. They let others walk all over them. Ask students what might happen if Shrinkers behave in a passive manner. Help students understand that although Shrinkers avoid conflict, they never really achieve their goals.

The best of both Blasters and Shrinkers, Me's know what they want and are not afraid to ask for it. However, they consider other people's feelings and rights as well. Me's say what they feel but in such a way that others can listen to them. They know they can't have what they want all the time but the best way to try is to work with others.

BEST is a way to help people act more like a Me rather than a Blaster or a Shrinker. It stands for

B—**B**ody posture: standing up straight, being confident in yourself but not arrogant.

E—**E**ye contact: looking the person directly in the eye, communicating openly.

S—**S**peech: using appropriate language and saying what you really feel.

T—**T**one of voice: using a calm voice, not whispering or shouting.

Teachers may wish to bring up cultural variations in BEST behaviors with their class. For example, discuss differences of eye contact and help students discriminate where and with whom different types of eye contact (posture, etc.) are most and least useful. Have students think of situations where they could use BEST. If they are having difficulty, think of a situation you had (or make one up) and model how you use BEST. Generate several scenarios and have students act out Blaster, Shrinker, and Me behaviors. (Feel free to generate new labels for the behavior with your class, as well.) When some students are role playing, assign others to watch them and give feedback on the four components of BEST. Practice can continue until improvement is noticed, and then others can have a turn.

Older students find the BEST skills relevant but are less likely to relate to the Blaster, the Shrinker, and the Me. They can generate examples of "too much" and "too little" BEST behavior, however, and then create their own labels. It is often useful to raise BEST in the context of a common class or group problem, such as talking to friends, dating, entering a group, job and other interviews, or starting new situations like camp or after-school clubs or sports.

Practice Activities for BE YOUR BEST

Following are additional activities to help students at all grade levels periodically practice BE YOUR BEST. They can be modified for specific groups of students who can discuss them, role play, and/or write about the situations and possible responses.

1. You spot your best friend coming out of a movie theater with another friend. Earlier in the day she told you she had to visit her aunt. You are feeling hurt. How should you handle this situation?

   a. I would not say anything to her because she might get angry with me.

   b. I would mention it to her in order to hear what she had to say.

   c. I would call her later and really let her have it for leaving me out. I may also ignore her for a few days and tell my friends to ignore her too.

2. A classmate borrowed two dollars from you and hasn't paid you back. It has been three weeks. How should you handle this situation?

   a. I would give him a piece of my mind and tell him that if he does not pay, he'll be sorry.

   b. I would not bother him and hope that he pays one of these days.

   c. I would remind him again and ask him when he will have the money.

For the following situations, students can indicate whether the person is acting like a Blaster, a Shrinker, or a Me. If they think that the person is acting like a Blaster or a Shrinker, they can role play a Me. If the person is a Me, ask students to think of other ways of acting like a Me for the situation.

1. John has been bothered by a boy in his class, who, for some reason, keeps picking on him. John sees the other boy coming.

He quickly starts walking in the other direction to avoid him. How is John acting? What else could he do?

2.   Marie's mother has been very angry at her lately. Today Marie forgot to take out the garbage and her mother grounded her for two days. Marie had been looking forward to a sleepover that night. She went to her mother, apologized, and offered to help with some cleaning. She also promised to leave a note on her desk to remind herself about taking the garbage out next time. How is Marie acting? What else could she do?

Additional examples can be created and practiced periodically to assist students in maintenance and transfer of the BE YOUR BEST skill.

4. FIG TESPN: A FORMAT FOR SOCIAL DECISION MAKING

Students already know many simple cause-effect relationships. . . .
Our primary goal is to help them progress from one-shot thinking
toward precise processing, so they can make refined analyses of any
relationships or situations that may be important to them, now and in
the future. (75, p. 70)

FIG TESPN is an acronym for the sequence of steps that guide
students through the process of social decision making and problem
solving. (See Table 4–1.) It provides a centralizing concept for students
to understand the steps as a whole process to engage in when confronted
with a problem or decision. The unique "name," FIG TESPN, is also a
mnemonic that reinforces memory. In addition, it is a convenient
prompt for teachers to use; for example, they can ask a student, "How
can FIG TESPN help you with this problem?"

The following lesson is designed to introduce students to the social
decision-making and problem-solving format. Ideally, it should be used
after the introduction and reinforcement of the readiness activities. It is
designed to stand on its own, however, and can be introduced at any
time.

When introducing a social decision-making lesson, it is important to
make clear to students that it is the activity being engaged in. Social
decision-making activities are different from academic tasks and both
teaching methods and student participation may be different. If possible,
schedule social decision-making lessons and activities on a regular basis,
especially during the introduction of FIG TESPN.

Table 4–1
FIG TESPN, Social Decision Maker

1. **FEELINGS** are your cue to problem solve.

2. **IDENTIFY** the issue.

3. **GUIDE** your self with a *goal*.

4. **THINK** of many possible things to do.

5. **ENVISION** end results for each option.

6. **SELECT** your best solution.

7. **PLAN** the procedure and anticipate roadblocks.

8. **NOTICE** what happened and remember it for next time.

The objectives of the FIG TESPN lesson are—

- To introduce students to the social decision-making and problem-solving steps.
- To provide students with a centralizing concept so that the social problem-solving steps can be remembered as a whole rather than as discrete steps.
- To provide students and teachers with a prompt for problem solving.

PROCEDURE

1. Prepare handouts of the FIG TESPN steps to give to all students (see Table 4–1).

2. Prepare a large poster of the FIG TESPN steps and place it in the classroom before the lesson to stimulate curiosity and serve as a prompt at a later time.

3. Tell students: The purpose of today's lesson is to introduce FIG TESPN, but I am not really sure who or what FIG TESPN is. FIG TESPN helps you solve problems and helps you figure out how to do things in the best way possible. FIG helps you use your own resources and abilities rather than doing it for you. FIG helps you think before

acting. FIG helps you decide the best thing to do to get what you want. FIG comes on the scene when feelings become strong and people have difficulty deciding what to do. (FIG TESPN = social decision making)

4. Generate from students examples of who FIG TESPN might be like. If they are having difficulty, discuss who provides guidance and helps others succeed without acting directly for them. If students cannot generate examples, prompt them with examples such as sports coaches, managers, movie characters, rock concert producers.

5. Encourage students to develop their own image of who FIG TESPN is like. Have them discuss this with the class.

6. Distribute FIG TESPN handouts. Explain that FIG can help them solve problems by reminding them to go through the eight steps and ask themselves these questions. Have students read the FIG TESPN steps and review relevant vocabulary and concepts.

7. Model a problem-solving situation using FIG's steps. Provide a semipersonal situation in which you had to solve a problem, to make a decision, or had a conflict with someone.

8. Assign students to think about situations in which FIG TESPN's questions could be helpful to them. Review these situations at the beginning of the next lesson.

ACTIVITIES

It is important for students to be actively involved with FIG TESPN; the following activities strongly reinforce the concept and personalize it.

1. Have students draw pictures or computer-generated images of FIG TESPN.

2. Have students write stories about FIG TESPN—for example, how FIG came to be, how FIG helped solve someone's problem.

3. Have a poster of the FIG TESPN steps in the room for students to refer to in subsequent lessons and/or when spontaneous problems arise.

4. Have students draw comic strips involving FIG TESPN.

5. Show the Disney version of the film *Pinocchio* and discuss comparisons between FIG TESPN and Jiminy Cricket.

6. Give a writing assignment with a beginning (feeling and problem) and an end. Have students fill in the middle of the story using FIG TESPN.

   For example, a new student is feeling nervous about being accepted by others and making friends (Feelings). He or she doesn't know how to go about making friends (Issue). He or she really wants to make friends (Goal). In the end, the student has a small group of close friends but is still excluded by the "cool" students (Notice what happened).

   The assignment is to have the main character in the story think of things to do, envision outcomes, select a solution, plan it, and do it, making the beginning and ending of the story consistent with the example.

7. Use cards with pictures of children in social situations to stimulate story-telling skills and to practice problem solving. Students can tell alternative stories, apply FIG TESPN in various ways, and arrange the cards to make increasingly elaborate, interconnected stories (see Appendix B—*Picture Arrangement Story Telling* by Tobias, Friedlander, and Elias).

Tips for Teaching FIG TESPN Most Effectively

1. Encourage students to be imaginative in their conception of FIG. To ensure that students develop their own images of FIG TESPN, try to avoid priming them with preconceived images. This will enhance retention and use.

2. Avoid referring to FIG as "he" or "she" because FIG should be universal.

3. At a later time, FIG will become a prompt for decision making and problem solving. For example, you could ask, "How could FIG help you with this?"

4. Here is an example of how eventually one can use FIG TESPN. In the following dialogue, a teacher is working with a class of students who have been introduced to FIG TESPN. Note how the teacher uses the techniques in Chapter 2, especially those in Table 2–2, to build students' skills.

Teacher: Class, we seem to have a problem today that I'm feeling a little confused about. We need to review for the test but I also was hoping to do some fun projects. I wonder if FIG TESPN could help us with this. Let's see . . . F . . . feelings. Well, I guess I said that I felt confused about what to do . . . I also will feel disappointed if we don't get to do the fun things I had planned . . . I also would feel a little guilty if I didn't help you review for the test. Do any of you have feelings about this problem?

Tommy: I want to do the fun stuff.

Teacher: Okay, but that's a goal. Do you have any *feelings* about this?

Tommy: I feel that we should do some review and then do the projects.

Teacher: That might be a good option and we'll think of things to do in a minute, but I'm still kind of wondering how you feel about this.

Tommy: I hate reviewing for tests, we already know the stuff and we never get to do anything fun.

Teacher: Okay, that's great, now we have a feeling. Tommy is feeling angry about having to do a review. Any other feelings?

Tanya: I feel happy that we might get to do fun stuff.

Teacher: Good, "happy" is another feeling.

Estevan: I'm a little nervous about the test.

Teacher: "Nervous." You are coming up with terrific feeling words. Any more feelings? . . . Okay, now we want to identify the issue. So what's the problem?

Sara: We want to do the fun stuff but we have to review for the test.

Teacher: "We want to do fun stuff but we have to review for the test." That's one way to say what the issue is. Any others?

Lauren: Why can't we just do the fun stuff?

Teacher: I'm glad you're thinking of things to do, but hold onto that idea for just a couple minutes until we get to that step. So what's our goal?

Andy: To do fun stuff.

Teacher: Okay, that's one goal, but we have talked about my goal of reviewing for the test. Since we are all part of the same class, we need a goal we can all agree on.

Andy: We can study and then do fun stuff.

Teacher: That's technically a "thing to do" but maybe you can rephrase that as a goal.

Andy: To study and also do fun stuff.

Teacher: Great, now that sounds like a goal to me. Does everybody agree with this goal? . . . Let's see, F—feelings, I—identify the issue, G—goal, T—what does T stand for again?

Kim: (Looking at the poster on the wall) Think of many possible things to do.

Teacher: Let's list them on the board. One . . .

Tommy: Do the fun stuff.

Teacher: Okay (writes this on the board). Another thing . . .

Ryan: Study for 20 minutes and then do fun stuff for 20 minutes.

Teacher: Great (writes this on the board). Something else . . . Remember, part of our goal is to study, but we didn't say how yet.

Tom: Maybe we could do the review at home and just do the fun stuff here.

Teacher: (Writes this on the board) Okay . . . how about some more things?

Samara: Do the fun things and those kids who need help could come after school.

Teacher: Okay that's great. We have four different things we can do. Next, we want to do what?

Charlotte: Envision!

Teacher: Right! So the first suggestion was to do the fun stuff. If we do the fun stuff, what do you envision happening?

Charlotte: We'll fail the test because we didn't review.

Teacher: Okay, that might happen. What else might happen? . . . Well, would we meet our goal of "to study and do fun stuff"?

Charlotte: No, because we only did fun stuff.

Teacher: Okay, anything else about this option?

Linda: I'd be happy if we did fun stuff.

Teacher: Okay, that's great. I'm glad you reminded us that it's always important to keep in mind the feelings that we have about the various things we think of doing. Let's see, the next option is to study for 20 minutes and then do fun staff for 20 minutes.

John: We'd meet our goal.

Teacher: Yes, we might. Anything else?

Louise: What if we needed more than 20 minutes to study?

Teacher: You are way ahead of me. That would be a roadblock to this option, wouldn't it? Well, let's keep that in mind. What else do you envision happening?

Louise: We could have fun.

Teacher: Okay, we could have some fun. Next option, review at home and do fun stuff here. What do you envision?

Barbara: Maybe when we get home we won't understand something.

Pat: I already have too much homework.

Howard: I'd rather review on my own and my father can help me.

Teacher: Great. Okay . . . anything else?

Kendall Well, what's the fun stuff you said we were going to do?

Teacher: I'll show you later if this ends up being part of our plan, but for now, let's try to work with all of FIG TESPN. Okay, any more visions? . . . The last thing we thought of doing was to have fun here and some kids who need help come after school. What might happen?

Tom: I'm not coming after school.

Teacher: Okay, some students might not come after school for help. What else?

Sara: I can't come after school because I have dance, but I don't need to come anyway.

Teacher: Okay, what you said brings up another thing that might happen. Some students might not be able to come after school; and we would need a way to decide who should come and who should not. Anything else? . . . Now we want to "S" . . .

Samara: Solve it!

Teacher: Good. "Solve it," or select our best solution. What do you think?

Samara: 20 minutes for fun and 20 minutes for review.

Mike: Forget the whole thing.

Lauren: That wasn't one of the things we thought of doing!

Teacher: Let's quickly review the things we thought of doing and what we envisioned happening. (Teacher reviews this.) Well, which one seems like our best solution?

Diego: Studying for 20 minutes and having fun for 20 minutes.

John: If we didn't have to do this stupid FIG TESPN we could've already been done studying.

Teacher: You know, you are really coming up with great points. Taking time to think and problem solve sometimes can be a pain, can't it? Sometimes it seems easier just to rush out there and do something instead of thinking it through first. Well, if you didn't help me think this through, I would have just said we need to review for the test and it would be too bad if we didn't have time to do the fun activities. But because we were able to think it through, it seems reasonable to me to review for half the time and do our fun activities for half the time. What do you think about using FIG TESPN to help us think through the problem?

Irving: I guess it was worth doing.

Clifton: I like using FIG—it helps me all the time.

Teacher: I'm happy to hear this! So, what's our plan?

Myra: Next period, we'll review and then do fun stuff.

Agnes: Maybe we could review by playing Jeopardy.

Teacher: Yes, that's something we didn't even think of, having fun while we study. I would like some volunteers to work with me to make up a Jeopardy game while the rest of you go over your notes and the chapter. Next period, we'll review the questions from the chapter and any questions you have. After that, we'll play Jeopardy.

Hyun Hee: Does Jeopardy count as review or fun time?

Teacher: Let me think . . . we are going to put things from the chapter into the Jeopardy game, so Jeopardy counts as review. But if the 20 minutes of review time ends and we are in the middle of a game, you can have the choice of continuing or doing the other activities I had planned. Can you anticipate any potential roadblocks? . . . And what is the last step in FIG TESPN, what does "N" stand for?

Maureen: Notice what happened.

Teacher: Good! At the end of the next period, we'll see how our plan worked because we may want to use it again sometime. All of you really did a great job of problem solving and coming to a decision. You know, I feel much less confused than I did when we started. I think we all should use FIG TESPN more often!

Subsequent lessons can involve guided rehearsal and practice, videotapes, written assignments, or real-life decisions and problems

68

encountered by students. For guided rehearsal and practice, present a problem common to students, such as peer conflict, being left out of a game, peer pressure to engage in a dangerous activity. Videotapes of some public television programs are also useful to analyze, using the TVDRP technique discussed in Chapter 2, Students can focus on one or more of the problems presented and discuss additional options or outcomes.

In the early stages of teaching FIG TESPN, it can be helpful to present all the steps and follow through from start to finish with a problem or decision, but with a particular focus and emphasis on one of the steps. The following guidelines for each step will be helpful.

Feelings are your cue to problem solve:

Feelings are the first step in problem solving because they provide a cue that something needs to be done. It is important to be aware of feelings and identify them. Have students generate a feelings vocabulary to help expand their awareness. Teach students to identify feelings in themselves and in others (review of the BEST behaviors can be useful here) through facial expression, body posture, voice, etc. A fun exercise is to play feelings charade; a student picks a feeling from a hat, acts it out, and others guess what it is.

Identify the issue:

Putting a problem into words is the first step in solving it. It is important to identify the problem and sort it out from other problems or feelings that may be occurring. Having students verbalize a problem is another technique for fostering impulse control through self-verbalization. At this point, if students come up with what seem to be problems that are irrelevant to a situation, do not censor or direct them to the "correct" problem. Allow them to continue through with the subsequent social problem-solving (SPS) steps. At some point, they may see that their solution does not address the problem as stated. Then, go back and reformulate the problem.

For example, two students had a fight. The teacher asks what the problem is. Tom says the problem is that John is a jerk. When Tom attempts to develop goals and options to deal with this, he may see that regardless of what his goal or solution is, he is not addressing the fact that John is a jerk. At that time, the teacher may help Tom reformulate the problem—for example, "John keeps teasing me."

Guide yourself with a goal:

Have students define what a goal is (for example, a specific thing you want to accomplish or have happen). Explain that goals give us direction so that we can work for something. Help students identify analogies or other examples of "goals" (e.g., in sports; rudders on boats; destinations; targets; bulls-eyes). Clarifying our goals enables us to develop plans to reach them. It is important for students to develop reasonable and reachable goals. It also may be necessary to identify subgoals; a student who wants to improve a grade in science first must complete daily assignments for the current week. Having students define general goals for themselves and discussing them can be a worthwhile activity in itself.

Think of many possible things to do:

Students generally do not recognize that there is more than one way to reach a goal. Teach them how to brainstorm (which involves writing down everything they can think of relevant to the problem). When brainstorming, it is important not to be critical in the initial stages because outrageous options may stimulate thought about more realistic ones. After brainstorming, go through the options and refine or combine them. At this point, refrain from rejecting options based on their potential outcomes. Wait for the next step to help students understand that the option may have unpleasant outcomes for them. Creative thinking exercises such as generating unusual uses for common objects are also helpful "starters" if your thinkers are a bit "stuck."

Envision end results for each option:

Discuss with students the importance of anticipating the consequences of actions. Explain that for every action there is a consequence. Have students generate examples of actions and consequences. Encourage them to think of several consequences for each action or option; the use of flow charts or webs can make this more graphic. You may also wish to develop a rating system—from positive to negative—to evaluate potential outcomes for each option.

Select your best solution:

When encouraging students to select their best solution, refer to the original problem and goal. Make sure that the solution addresses these factors. It may be necessary to rethink one or several of the previous steps.

When formulating a solution, several options can be combined. For example, if the goal is to pass a test, the solution may be to develop a study schedule, to ask a friend to study with you, and to outline all the chapters.

Plan the procedure and anticipate roadblocks:

Planning can be a difficult step for students, especially if they are not accustomed to thinking in a deliberate manner before acting. Use relevant analogies to reinforce its importance: the planning that goes into a space shuttle launch, the planning necessary for a family vacation, planning how and when to ask someone for a date. Plans have at least four components: Who, What, When, and Where. Be sure plans involve each of these components; introduce issues of timing and coordination into the planning process of adolescents.

Notice what happened and remember it for next time:

This step is important to help students understand that despite their best efforts, their plans might not meet with success. Teach them to self-evaluate and, if necessary, to rethink the problem or decision. You may have to engage students in another FIG TESPN, using the outcome of the initial FIG TESPN to help define a new problem to be solved. Be sure to start with students' feelings about the problem not being solved or the decision not working out.

APPLICATIONS

FIG TESPN also has applications to everyday classroom activities, especially in the areas of literature and social studies and classroom behavior. These applications serve as potent and frequent reinforcers or extenders of the FIG TESPN thinking framework. (In addition, there are obvious parallels of FIG TESPN with the scientific method.) The following examples illustrate how to apply FIG TESPN relatively informally to common classroom activities. Chapter 5 contains a more extensive discussion and ideas for creating social decision-making-based lesson plans in these and other areas.

Literature

When reading a story, students can apply FIG TESPN to problems the characters encounter or decisions they make. Be sure to start with a discussion of how the characters feel about a situation. This requires a high degree of inferential thinking at times. Nevertheless, these inferences can be grounded in the material students are reading. Issues of authors' styles, paraphrasing, and use of language can be highlighted with adolescents and preadolescent gifted and talented students. Students can then identify the problem and goal in their own words, which also facilitates comprehension. They can see, too, that there may be other options characters in the story can take, and they can discuss these options and potential outcomes. If the character had a plan, students can also evaluate it. They can analyze the authors' purposes in crafting plans as they did, and meeting certain outcomes. Issues of dramatic tension, irony, and conflict can easily be illustrated. Finally, it may be interesting for students to infer what happens after the story ends. Perhaps they can discuss, outline, or write sequels.

These topics can either be discussed in class or carried out as written assignments. Another type of assignment or discussion that has been used successfully involves students reading or hearing part of a story and using FIG TESPN to complete it. Or, students can be given the beginning and end of a story and be required to make up a middle. This alternative is useful for illustrating the different options that can be used to reach an end.

Social Studies

FIG TESPN can be used in social studies to analyze current events. For example, if there is unrest in a certain country, students can read a newspaper or *Weekly Reader* article and then answer guided questions:

- How do the citizens of this country feel?
- What problems are they having?
- What is an important goal for them?
- What are several ways they could reach their goal?
- What might happen if they try these methods?
- What do you think is the best thing for them to do?
- How could they do it?
- What might happen after they do it? Do you think they can be successful? If so, why were they successful? If they were not successful, what else could they do?

This format can also be applied to historical situations. For example, FIG TESPN can guide a discussion of why the Pilgrims came to America.

How did the Pilgrims feel about religious persecution? How did they arrive at the decision to leave England? Instead of coming to America, what else could they have done? What would have happened if they had chosen one of these other solutions? These and other questions inspired by FIG TESPN are likely to lead students to do additional research and gather needed information to better enable them to generate realistic answers. Yet their engagement in the process allows much of their learning to be self-directed, discovery-oriented, and likely to be of lasting benefit as they learn how to "think about" and learn about history. (See Elias and Clabby [31] for additional suggestions on using FIG TESPN in language arts and social studies.)

Everyday Interpersonal Application

FIG TESPN can be applied to everyday interpersonal problems or decisions encountered by students. Guided questioning by the teacher can facilitate the resolution of peer conflicts and address persistent problems. The use of FIG TESPN can alleviate the anxiety generated by potential future problems by helping students develop a plan to cope with them.

If students are not getting along or there is a crisis, they can be taken aside as a class, in a small group, in dyads, or individually, and guided through the FIG TESPN steps. It is important for the teacher to function as a facilitator rather than a problem solver; in other words, the teacher does not tell the student what he or she should do, but rather helps the student focus on how to solve the problem by carefully thinking through all aspects of it. The facilitative questioning strategies discussed in Chapter 2 apply perfectly here.

Students who are in a highly aroused emotional state will be resistant to discussing anything in a positive manner. It may be necessary to help them Keep Calm and practice BEST. Before initiating any discussion, it may also be helpful to have them write down what happened. This will allow time for the intensity of their emotions to abate and to introduce the cognitive component to solving their problem, which will reduce impulsivity.

FIG TESPN also can be used to address low-level, everyday, but persistent, problems. For example, a student may be coming to class late regularly. The teacher can indicate to the student that this is a problem that needs to be solved. In this instance, the teacher may indicate her/his feelings, the problem, and the goal, and require the student to generate options for solving the problem. The teacher may include certain incentives as part of the plan—coming to class on time every day for a week earns a choice of reward such as special activities, free time, or a classroom privilege; coming to class late two days in a row earns a detention. Forgetting homework, disruptions in class, and other common problems also can be dealt with. The teacher may facilitate problem solving and at times offer suggestions, but it is important to keep in mind that the more the student engages in the problem-solving process, the greater the chance for success. Teacher-generated solutions too often fail to have the desired effect and do not teach the student how to solve problems independently.

FIG TESPN can also alleviate many stresses that students encounter in school. FIG TESPN can help students organize and plan for studying for a test; FIG TESPN can prepare students for a transition to a new grade or school; FIG TESPN can also help students cope with potential social stresses such as trying out for a sports team or making new friends. In all these situations, it is important to guide students through the steps using a facilitative approach.

WHEN AND HOW TO USE THESE ACTIVITIES

The format and activities in Chapters 3 and 4 have been used with middle grade students and have been adapted for use with high school and elementary students as well. Chapters 1 and 2 addressed ideas for where and how to "fit" these into school routines. Because the activities draw from school- and student-based experiences within the common framework of FIG TESPN, Keep Calm, and other related skills, their combination of stability and freshness allows for successful use of the approach and activities over a period of years. As students mature, so does their use of social decision making—and so does FIG TESPN! Chapters 5 and 6 contain specific guidelines for tailoring and adapting the basic framework given in Chapters 3 and 4 to a variety of commonly encountered educational situations.

5. INCORPORATING SOCIAL DECISION-MAKING ACTIVITIES IN THE CLASSROOM

> An effort to treat children with respect is likely to result in the creation of opportunities for them to talk, reason (with authority), and consider the long-term consequences of their actions and make explicit and discuss the values, codes, and long-term considerations that should guide those actions. In the course of doing this, children will practice complex cognitive activities. They will, for example, imagine and anticipate possible long-term consequences of their actions. They will imagine barriers to achieving their goals. They will consider a broad range of possibly conflicting consequences of their actions and choose between them. They will develop confidence in their ability to handle ideas, come to think of themselves as individuals capable of handling such ideas, and who have a right to opinions of their own. They will come to think of authority as something that is open to reason. (63, pp. 31–32)

This chapter and the one that follows address ways in which educators can bring into everyday school routines a variety of activities that strengthen social decision making. Chapter 5 provides approaches for infusing social decision making in the following areas: health and family life education; projects or reports for any subject area; as a format for group guidance, class sharing, or social life skills instruction; individual students' academic difficulties; and as a structure and clarification for decision making involving educational teams, as well as teachers and parents. Chapter 6 addresses ways to match social decision-making approaches to the needs of specific populations or subgroups in the schools. Taken together, Chapters 5 and 6 provide a grid or framework for planning and tailoring school-based efforts to promote thoughtful social decision making.

HEALTH AND FAMILY LIFE EDUCATION

To an increasing degree, health educators are identifying sound decision making around health-related behaviors as an overarching

75

instructional goal (43, 48, 62). Social decision making—including skills related to self-control and social awareness and group participation—is well suited to serve as a basic, integrative, developmental framework for health-related decision making. It is most useful when "health" is defined to include physical, social, community, familial, or psychological aspects, as is recommended by the National Professional School Health Organizations (57). While there are many effective ways to infuse social decision making into health education, we will focus on the following: (a) FIG TESPN as a guide for health-related discussions, (b) a TVDRP format (see pp. 40, 43–46, 78–79) for covering health topics, and (c) a language arts format for generating critical thinking and discussion around health issues.

FIG TESPN: Tackling the Problem of Substance Abuse

Like all health-related issues, substance use and abuse must be labeled for students as reflecting both personal and interpersonal decisions. Every health behavior has effects on the self and on others (friends, classmates, parents, siblings, other relatives); these effects must be carefully separated, specified, and examined.

Any given substance—cigarettes, chewing tobacco, beer, wine, hard liquor, pills, cocaine, crack, heroin, amphetamines, barbiturates—can be introduced as a topic and discussed using FIG TESPN as a framework. One way to open such a discussion is, "How do you feel (or, would you feel) if someone asks you to try ___?" Different ways of thinking through the problem can be written on the board or on paper; possible consequences and obstacles of trying different solutions and plans can be tried out through guided practice and rehearsal.

A more general way of introducing such discussions with younger students is to ask, "How do you feel about ___ (e.g., cigarettes)?" "What problems do you see for people who smoke?" Then goals can be set, alternatives to smoking discussed, and plans made. As part of the last step in FIG TESPN, students can be asked to make public commitments about not smoking, an effective public health technique. Teachers find it useful to ask youngest students to discuss how FIG TESPN would advise people who are thinking about smoking or using alcohol or drugs. "How do you think FIG feels about smoking? Why? What does smoking do to your body?" "What problems would FIG point out?" "How would FIG want that person's health to turn out?" "What would FIG suggest someone do instead of smoke?" "If someone bothered you to smoke, how would FIG want you to handle it?"

FIG TESPN also is useful for discussing the related, delicate problem of what to do when a friend or loved one is involved in some form of substance abuse. This is a volatile issue, especially when a parent is involved (see Chapter 6 for suggestions).

Across all health-related FIG TESPN applications, the most important skills to emphasize are guiding oneself through clear goals and envisioning a variety of outcomes or consequences. As discussions take place, the following incomplete sentences can be written on the board and used to keep track of ideas that students express:

"When people _____ , their goal is to _____ ."

Examples can include "When people eat vegetables, their goal is to please their parents"; "When people drink beer, their goal is to be part of the group"; "When people spend time with their families, their goal is to have fun being with them."

The link of actions, goals, and consequences can then be made by creating dittos that look something like this:

If my goal is to _____ , then some things that can help me get there and not hurt me or others are

_____

_____

_____

_____

For each goal, a "menu" or personal workbook can be created that students can review and keep available throughout the year to add to or look over for ideas. Many times teachers find it useful to provide a set of goals that are commonly implicit or hidden reasons that contribute to high-risk health behaviors. These include—

- to fit into a group
- to please one's friends
- to relieve "pressure"
- to imitate sports stars
- to feel good or happy
- to imitate television, video, or music personalities
- to get revenge on parents (or others).

By placing these goals in the format of the ditto, the idea of using risky health behaviors to reach these goals loses some of its plausibility, as well as some of its secrecy.

Many schools use existing health promotion or substance abuse prevention curricula or programs. Teachers find that FIG TESPN is highly consistent with virtually all of them because it provides a consistent framework for thinking and decision making that can be applied across individual topic areas. The resulting curricular continuity and synergy makes it more likely that instructional goals can be met. Examples of health programs and curricula related to substance abuse that articulate well with FIG TESPN include *Growing Healthy* (56), *Life Skills Training* (8), *AIDS Prevention* (16), the *Nutrition Education Curriculum* (19), the *Minnesota Heart Health Program* (40), and *Programs to Advance Teen Health (PATH)* (58). Self-control, social awareness, and group participation skills also are valuable adjuncts to these and related curricula (31).

TVDRP: Addressing the Transition to Adolescence

The topic of transition to adolescence encompasses many different aspects of health; the situations faced by students as they negotiate their transitions lead to innumerable decisions and problems. The TVDRP format is an engaging way to organize a series of lessons relating to the transition. The video material can come from a variety of sources; many public television stations broadcast excellent series (e.g., *Degrassi Junior High*), and companies such as the Agency for Instructional Technology (1) are constantly developing and updating relevant series (e.g., Self-Incorporated). If screened carefully, contemporary movies or television shows can be used (e.g., *The Bill Cosby Show*). Either a video that touches upon a variety of problem areas, several that focus on specific topics, or a combination can be used. In each case, the video provides a springboard for focused discussion and rehearsal, practice, and other followup activities.

Table 5–1 contains an instructional outline, based on a TVDRP approach. The video used is a general one that introduces a variety of difficulties and hassles experienced by Jonathan over the course of a brief period of time, all tied to his "growing up." This outline is designed to reflect the purposes indicated. Subsequent lessons, some using TVDRP, others using FIG TESPN, and others using the language arts-based approach to be described next, would focus on specific topics generated in the discussion. Clearly, the TVDRP approach can articulate well with existing curriculum materials.

Language Arts and Social Decision Making:
Partners in Promoting Health

Students enjoy reading stories; stories are a valuable way to build language skills, encourage thoughtful social decision making, and apply both sets of skills to health and family life issues. Also, a wider range of students find stories more engaging than they do more didactic and text-based health-related presentations. Students can read and discuss stories from the overall FIG TESPN perspective presented in Table 2–7, or they can be asked to focus on (a) how different characters were feeling; (b) how the author conveyed those feelings; (c) clarifying characters' goals, (d) exploring various options and consequences—both those presented and those not presented; and (e) designing alternative endings. Stories can be read through or discussions can be held at appropriate points, perhaps anticipating certain choices and decisions.

Examples of stories and topics include the following:

For young readers:

- *Little Rabbit's Loose Tooth* (dental) by Lucy Bate
- *Bea and Mrs. Jones* (the world of work) by Amy Schwartz
- *The Sleep Book* (sleep and rest) by Dr. Seuss
- *So That's How I Was Born* (conception and birth) by Dr. Richard Brooks
- *Gregory the Terrible Eater* (nutrition) by Mitchell Shermat
- *Arthur's Eyes* (glasses, vision, handicaps) by Marc Brown

For middle schoolers:

- *My Life in the Seventh Grade* (general problems) by Mark Geller
- Assorted books by Judy Blume, Mary Stolz, Miriam Chaikin, John Fitzgerald, Roald Dahl, Erich Kastner (each author has written about a variety of problem areas and issues)

For high schoolers:

- Bill Cosby's books (*Fatherhood, Time Flies, Love and Marriage*) offer insights and humor, as well as opportunities to check his views and suggest alternative perspectives about family living, parenting, raising teenagers, and parents' own adult development and aging.

In addition, short articles from magazines, such as *Highlights, Humpty Dumpty, World*, can be useful springboards for langauge arts lessons. Appendix A contains an example of how independent story-reading assignments can be crafted to focus on key decision-making skills, using original, interrelated stories for middle schoolers based on the theme, "Think Now for Later" (26). Each set of stories can lead to writing assignments and/or whole-class or small-group discussions, based on structured questions or general thought essays.

Table 5–1
TVDRP Introduction to Transition to Adolescence
Becoming an Adolescent—New Feelings, New Decisions

Purpose:

1. To help students acknowledge, label, and share the new feelings they are experiencing as they enter into adolescence.
2. To help students acknowledge, label, and share the kinds of problems they are now facing as they enter into adolescence.
3. To help students see that these new feelings and the new problems that arise give opportunities for making decisions.
4. To introduce the concept of understanding the goals students have in a given situation.

Instructional Outline

1. *Prepare*
   a. Elicit some of the changes involved in becoming an adolescent by asking students to share some problems they have had to deal with since they started (fifth, sixth, seventh) grade, or to share some changes in their feelings. OR
   b. Assign students to read about some of the changes involved in becoming an adolescent before any discussion.

2. *Review*
   a. Ask students to recall any previous class work on this topic.

3. *Orient*
   a. Make the point that handling the feelings, problems, and opportunities that go along with becoming an adolescent involves *making decisions*. Ask students what it means to be a *thoughtful decision maker* and list these qualities on the board.

Table 5–1 (Continued)

b. Make the point that feelings and problems don't "make" us do things—*we* decide and *we* choose. We can do a better job of choosing if we are thoughtful decision makers. (If students have learned social decision making and/or FIG TESPN, review these skills with them and point out their relevance to adolescent decisions.)

c. Uses examples from health and personal care (care of teeth, taking vitamins or medicine, smoking) and ask: "How do you decide whether or not to _____?"

4. *Focus*

a. Tell students that today they are going to watch a videotape about _____.

(For example, *What's Wrong With Jonathan?* from the Self-Incorporated series, is a 15-minute videotape about a boy who keeps encountering all kinds of minor hassles and starts to wonder, as others do, if there's something wrong with him.)

b. Ask half the students to focus on all the different problems Jonathan is having; ask the other half to focus on all the feelings Jonathan expresses.

5. *Show*

a. Show the videotape.

6. *Discuss*

a. Review the main events and sequence of the video.

b. Ask students to report Jonathan's problems; ask someone to list them on the board.

c. Ask students to report the feelings they noticed, and the signs of those feelings; ask a student to list these on the board.

d. Say that sometimes our feelings and problems make it confusing to figure out what to do. When this happens, we have to think about our goals—what we want to happen. Ask students how Jonathan felt during each problem and what his goal might be. What would their goals be if *they* were Jonathan?

7. *Rehearse and Practice*

a. Set up opportunities to rehearse how students might try to reach different goals if they were Jonathan. Give different actors a chance to try each situation. (If students know Be Your BEST or VENT [from Chapter 3] or other social skills prompts, encourage them to use them.)

b. Offer students the opportunity to talk about and rehearse and practice problems *they* have been facing. Assist the class by offering constructive feedback.

Table 5–1 (Continued)

8. *Summarize*
   a. Regardless of the stopping point in the lesson, elicit summaries of what has been happening and the main points learned; correct as needed. Prepare students for the next lesson.

9. *Continue*
   a. Plan followup activities, either focusing on one aspect of adolescent changes or on a range of changes. Encourage small group work and projects.
   b. Provide worksheets with different situations and ask students to list possible feelings and goals for different decisions. Ask students to work individually or in groups, and use decisions such as the following:
      • What time to go to sleep (early or late)
      • Whether to clean your room (yes or no)
      • Whether to smoke (yes or no)
      • How to handle all your energy (work or play)
      • How to handle it when a boy/girl you like ignores you (sad, angry, persistent)
      • Whether to take something from a store if your friends are also doing it (yes or no)
      • Whether to cheat on a test or copy someone else's work and hand it in (yes or no)
      • Whether to drink alcohol (yes or no)
      The format of the worksheet could ask about feelings and goals for *each possible decision* (e.g., "What would be your feelings and goals if you said, 'Yes, I will keep my room clean?' What would be your feelings and goals if you said, 'No, I won't keep my room clean?'"
   c. Hand out a sheet to help students keep track of feelings, problems, goals, decisions, and reasons for their chosen actions around problem situations that come up during the next day or two. These can be reviewed as part of the *presentation* and *review* sections of the next lesson.
   d. Assign a language arts followup activity (described in the text).

PLANNING AND CARRYING OUT PROJECTS AND REPORTS

The process of planning and carrying out projects and reports can engage and promote critical thinking, rather than rote procedures geared toward "getting finished." Especially among special education and disaffected students, as well as slow learners and gifted and talented, much is gained when students have a choice about (a) aspects of a topic to focus on, (b) where to look for information, and (c) how to present it.

Table 5–2 is a worksheet reprinted from a lesson plan for accomplishing these purposes (31, pp. 157–58). Taming Tough Topics recognizes that while a topic often must be determined by the teacher, at times there can, and should, be some latitude to explore aspects of that topic. Similarly, students are too often channeled toward a standard written report. This tends to lead to an excursion to an encyclopedia for some copying. For some students with poor writing skills, written reports can be a guaranteed—and unnecessary—turnoff.

What we have found is that, given some choice, students become more motivated to expend effort. Students in one special education class using Taming Tough Topics as a framework for studying Indians of New Jersey wanted to learn more about what happened to these native Americans, the sports they played, even the radio station they listened to. Students generated sources of information, including museums, sound filmstrips, and people of Indian ancestry. Their presentation formats ranged from a written interview with a Native American to a series of dioramas to a "period play"; older students also have created videos.

Typically, teachers review the worksheet with a group or an entire class, brainstorming answers to each question and writing them on the board. This engages students in a shared social decision-making process; this process continues as students select their preferences and then carefully plan and check their work before deciding that their final product is completed. One fascinating use of Taming Tough Topics has been around AIDS. As a means of gauging students' knowledge and concerns, educators have introduced the topic AIDS, and then engaged K–12 classes in discussions of various questions. Based on students' responses, developmentally and informationally appropriate assignments have been generated, ranging from a simple focus (What is it?) to the more philosophical (Why do people have to die from it?).

SOCIAL STUDIES INSTRUCTION

Among many perspectives for social studies (or social sciences) instruction, one that we have found highly engaging to students emphasizes how decisions have been, and continue to be, made in certain historical contexts. History is presented as a series of decisions made by individuals and groups, reflecting certain goals, options, consequences, plans, and lessons for the future. In short, FIG TESPN has been used as

Table 5–2
Taming Tough Topics

Name: _____ Class: _____ Date: _____

First: Define your problem and goal.

    1. What is the topic?

    2. What are some questions you would like to answer or learn about the topic?

Second: List alternative places to look for information.

    1. Write at least five possible places where you can look for information.

        a. _____
        b. _____
        c. _____
        d. _____
        e. _____

    2. Plan which ones you will try first.

    3. Who else can you ask for ideas if these do not work?

Third: List alternative ways to present the topic.

    1. Write at least three ways in which to present the topic. If it is a written report, write three ways to write it.

        a. _____
        b. _____
        c. _____

    2. Consider the consequences for each way, choose your best solution, and plan how you will do it.

Fourth: Make a final check, and fix what needs fixing.

    1. Does your presentation answer the topic and the questions you asked? Is it clear and neat? Is the spelling correct? Will others enjoy it?

a framework for analyzing historical and current events.

Successfully used outlines based on FIG TESPN can be found in Table 5–3 (31, pp. 163–64). These outlines can be modified for specific purposes (e.g., Haboush [39]) and linked with readings, further research (and Taming Tough Topics), and various types of projects. The social decision-making framework works well with social studies as taught at all levels (2). For young readers, books such as *Watch the Stars Come Out* by Riki Levinson (Reading Rainbow Library edition, by E. P. Dutton, 1985) contain stories related to historical periods (here, the immigration from Europe to the land of liberty) and complementary enrichment activities. At many points, FIG TESPN can be used to help students think more deeply about the issues. (For example, How did the immigrants feel about leaving their countries? What countries were they leaving? What contemporary problems made them want to leave? What problems would leaving bring about? What would have been their goals in leaving or staying? What were their options and how did they envision the results of each possibility? What plans did they have to make? What kinds of things got in their way at the last minute? How did they overcome the roadblocks? Once they arrived how did they feel? What problems did they encounter at the beginning? What were their first goals?) As needed, further reading and research could be assigned to help students find fact-based answers to these and related questions, in addition to checking their own thoughts.

Table 5–3
Thinking About Important Events

Name: _____ Class: _____ Date: _____

Events in History

1. What is the event that you are thinking about? When and where did it happen? Put the event into words as a problem.

2. What people or groups were involved in the problem? What were their different feelings and points of view about the problem? Try to put their goals into words

3. For each group, name some different decisions or solutions to the problem that the group members thought might help them reach their goals.

Table 5–3 (Continued)

4. For each solution, think of all the things that might have happened next. Think about short- and long-term consequences.

5. What were the final decisions? How were they made? By whom? Why? Do you agree or disagree? Why?

6. How was the solution carried out? What was the plan? What obstacles were met? How well was the problem solved? Why?

7. Rethink it. What would *you* have chosen to do? Why?

Current Events

1. What is the event that you are thinking about? When and where is it happening? Put the event into words as a problem.

2. What people or groups are involved in the problem? What are their different feelings and points of view about the problem? Try to put their goals into words.

3. For each group, name some different solutions to the problem that the group members think might help them reach their goals.

4. For each solution, think of all the things that might happen next. Think about short- and long-term consequences.

5. What do you think the final decision should be? How should it be made? By whom? Why?

6. Think of a plan to help you carry out your solution. What could you do to make your solution work?

7. Make a final check. What might happen that could keep your solution from working? Who might disagree with you? Why? What else could you do?

Beginning at about middle-school age, an exciting offshoot of the social decision-making approach is to have teams of students organize around using FIG TESPN as a framework to address and resolve genuine problems. These could be problems in the school, local community issues, or even larger problems of pollution, war and peace, world hunger, and lack of liberty. In the Berkeley Heights (New Jersey) school district, sixth graders addressed local environmental problems using the approaches suggested here and in the Application Phase of social decision making (31). The students' work received communitywide attention and recognition by the state legislature; it culminated in a Presidential Environmental Award, complete with a White House ceremony. Organizing students as problem-solving teams using FIG TESPN fits with and is complementary to many recent curricular initiatives related to the "global community and such topics as vandalism, poverty, education, world peace, terrorism, toxic wastes, future jobs, and the elderly" (20, 22, 47).

For high school students, a challenging extension of the middle-school approach is to participate in the nonpartisan Foreign Policy Association's "Great Decisions" series (729 Seventh Avenue, New York, NY 10019). Each year, a briefing book, activities book, bibliography, leadership handbook, and world map are developed around key topics. The materials are designed to provide information for discussion and to assist in developing school- and community-wide forums and communication with policymakers. Topics for 1990 include the following:

- U.S.S.R. and Eastern Europe: End of an Era?
- U.S., Europe, and Japan: Global Economy in Transition?
- Nicaragua and El Salvador: War or Peace in Central America?
- Vietnam, Cambodia, and the U.S.: Return Engagement?
- Third World Arms Bazaar: Disaster for Sale?
- United Nations: New Life for an Aging Institution?
- Palestinian Question: Is There a Solution?
- Global Warming and the Environment: Forecast Disaster?

The FIG TESPN framework can be easily used to conduct discussions based on the materials provided.

Finally, the use of *biography* is an excellent vehicle for teaching the influence of human decision making on history. Biographies of historic figures such as Martin Luther King, Jr., many presidents, explorers, inventors, and scientists such as Ben Franklin and Marie Curie bring to life certain periods. FIG TESPN can be used to discuss characters' feelings, goals, alternatives, and the like. Regardless of the type of format used, the focus is on building students' thinking abilities and social decision-making skills—essential for effective functioning in a sophisticated, twenty-first century society.

GROUP GUIDANCE, CLASS SHARING, AND LIFE SKILLS INSTRUCTION

A common element in group-guidance, class-sharing, and life-skills instruction is to have students keep track of concerns, problems, or difficulties they encounter and bring them to the group for sharing and discussion. To make it more likely that students do keep track of problems and to provide a consistent framework for thinking through these problems in a way that builds their social decision-making skills, educators can use a Problem Tracker (Table 5–4). This device is based on the Problem Diary, a technique for self-monitoring how well one handles stressful situations (31). The Problem Tracker outline can be modified to become a worksheet that allows students of any grade to write or depict situations they would like to bring to the attention of their group (or just to the instruction). The format uses an inductive, self-questioning procedure to help students think through their concerns or problems and move toward appropriate action. Teachers (and principals) of regular and special education students have found it useful to have Problem Trackers handy and direct students to fill them out when they are upset or troubled before talking to adults about a situation or their actions. Having students fill out the Tracker (or dictating their responses, if necessary) provides a buffer that allows for more thoughtful discussion. It also makes it clear that students are responsible for trying to solve their problems. By discussing Trackers regularly in groups, students become exposed to a consistent, inductive strategy for thinking through a range of problems and concerns. Discussions can be followed by guided rehearsal and practice of alternative actions students plan to take.

Table 5–4
The Problem Tracker

Name_____

Date_____

1. In this space, write (or draw) what it is that is bothering you or that was a problem for you this week. Try to include *who* is involved and *when* or *where* it is taking place.

2. What did you say and do? *or* What would you like to say and do?

3. What happened in the end? *or* What would you like to have happen?

4. So far, how easy or hard has it been for you to stay calm and under control when dealing with this problem? (circle one number)

1	2	3	4	5
very easy to control myself	pretty easy	so-so	pretty hard	very hard to control myself

5. How satisfied are you with the way you have been trying to solve the problem so far?

1	2	3	4	5
not at all	only a little	so-so	pretty satisfied	very, very satisfied

6. What do you like about what you have been doing so far?

7. What don't you like about what you have been doing so far?

8. What are some other ways you can handle the situation?

ADDRESSING STUDENTS' ACADEMIC DIFFICULTIES

Many students experience a common set of problems around organizing themselves to do their academic work. This has been found to be a particular issue in the transition of students into middle, junior high, or high schools (32). A variation of the Problem Tracker has been a valuable tool for teachers, counselors, and learning specialists to help individual students gradually learn to identify academic organizations and related problems and move toward solutions. The Self-Responsibility Worksheet (Table 5–5) was developed by the Improving Social Awareness-Social Problem Solving Project team (see Appendix B) in collaboration with dozens of teachers; it is presented in its most successful form, as used with students in grades 5–12. We encourage modifications as needed. Most critical, however, is to recognize the importance of several principles in the ultimate effective use of the worksheet:

1. Start simply to achieve initial success.
2. Old habits take time to modify and replace with positive work habits.
3. Communication of the plans derived from the worksheet to other educators and to parents can improve consistency and reduce students' frustration.
4. The "Other" spaces can be used to further tailor the worksheet.
5. Don't stop using the worksheet too soon. Many students still need its "prompt and cue" value to continue to be successful. Internalization and transfer of learning take considerable time.

Table 5–5
Self-Responsibility Worksheet

Name:_____ Date:_____

Homeroom Teacher: _____

1. Read the following list. Check the statements that apply to you:

Developing the Problems

_____ not doing homework
_____ forgetting to do homework
_____ coming to school late

Table 5–5 (Continued)

_____ coming to class late

_____ losing my books

_____ losing my pen or pencil

_____ not writing down homework assignments

_____ leaving completed homework in the locker or at home

_____ once I'm in class I can't find what I need

_____ my teachers tell me I get my homework half done

_____ I always forget or lose things that I need for gym

OTHER _____

OTHER _____

2. Read over the statements that you have checked. Which two or three things seem to get you into difficulty most *often*?

    a. _____

    b. _____

    c. _____

3. Which of these problem situations (from #2) would you most like to change? I want to change_____

_____

4. What is your goal? (How do you want things to be different?) My goal is to

5. Write about one time when this problem bothered you or got you into trouble.

6. What are some things you could have said or done *differently* so the problem would have been smaller or maybe not there at all? Write *at least three different* things you can think of.

Table 5–5 (Continued)

If I had said or done this   THEN this would have happened next.

7. Look at your answers to #2 and #6. Now, put together your best ideas and develop a step-by-step plan that will help you to reach your goal.

8. Look over your plan.

   a. What could happen to keep your plan from working?

   b. If these things happened, how would you handle it?

EDUCATIONAL TEAMS AND TEACHERS AND PARENTS

Thoughtful social decision making can often be disregarded when groups of educators or teachers and parents meet to discuss students. Everyone brings to these meetings individual perspectives, beliefs about learning and behavior, and histories of the child under discussion, as well as those of many similar (and different) children. Too often occurring under time constraints, these meetings are not as productive as they might be. Realistically, avoiding such meetings altogether can become easy.

As a means of structuring these meetings and providing a format for discussion that is likely to feature thoughtful social decision making, we have found the Educational Planner to be an essential tool (Table 5-6). Typically, each participant completes the planner before the meeting, or at least before the discussion. Then, the discussion begins by ensuring that there is a shared vision of the problem and goals before solutions are considered. Too often, plans are made but not implemented or followed through extensively because adults do not accept or believe in the problem as defined, the goals set, or the solutions proposed. The worksheet process also calls for consensus on realistic, implementable plans of action. By using the social decision-making process as adults, educators and parents can become more sensitive to and skilled in its use with students; they also come to realize and appreciate its many possible practical applications.

Table 5–6
The Educational Planner

Describe.
    Briefly describe the situation and the nature of the decision(s) to be made.

Analyze.
    How do you feel when you think about the situation? How do you think the child/members of the family/members of your team feel?

Clarify.
    What exactly are the decisions to be made? By what date? What about the situation is troublesome or difficult for you?

Focus.
    What would you like to see happen? Imagine the ideal decision and how things would work out for all involved.

Brainstorm.
    Think of as many ways as possible to solve this decision-making problem.

	Ideas	Consequences
1.	_____	_____
2.	_____	_____
3.	_____	_____
4.	_____	_____
5.	_____	_____
6.	_____	_____

Anticipate.
    For each of the ideas you listed, visualize what you think would happen as a result and fill in the spaces provided. Be sure to think about long- and short-term consequences and consequences for the various people involved—including yourself.

Table 5–6 (Continued)

Choose.
Take a good look at all the ideas and consequences. What do you think looks like the best thing (or things) to do? What will get you closest to your desired outcome(s)?

Plan.
What do you need to know, get, say, do, etc., to make the decision work? What is your time line?

Discuss.
If you think your ideas and plans are ready, arrange to discuss them with the other team members. If you are not comfortable with your ideas, take a fresh sheet and try to work things out on paper one more time. When you do meet with the team to discuss the situation, have all members bring their planner and use each of its points as a way to guide the discussion. Remember to try to find a discussion time when people are ready to sit and talk about things.

6. TAILORING THE USE OF SOCIAL DECISION MAKING TO DIFFERENT SCHOOL POPULATIONS

As our country's schools incorporate increasingly diverse student populations, the old definitions of excellence are challenged by the competing values, styles, and frames of intelligence of people from different origins. (49, p. 15)

At least 80 percent of the students in this country, like every other country in the world, have never acquired what you and I would agree is one of the major ingredients of being a well-educated person: the capacity to use their minds well. . . . To engage a mind in school, to get some students to be passionately engaged in school, is the heart of a good education. (54, pp. 25–26)

—Comments made at the Teachers College Centennial Symposium, "National Standards for American Education," November 19, 1988.

Social decision-making and problem-solving techniques have been applied to a variety of populations and for a variety of reasons—developing greater social competence, coping with academic stress, and solving interpersonal conflicts. FIG TESPN is a generic format that can be used across settings; for specific populations and purposes, however, its effectiveness can be enhanced through certain emphases, adaptations, and modifications. This chapter discusses issues to consider for tailoring social decision making for use with several different school populations—the learning disabled, the gifted and talented, students with attention deficits, the emotionally disturbed, and populations of difference.

LEARNING-DISABLED POPULATIONS

Students with learning disabilities often have deficits in social skills. They have difficulty reading nonverbal and other subtle social cues. Rejection by peers can compound feelings of failure that often are associated with academic frustration. A crucial area for these students, social skills development, is often included in the individualized education plan (IEP). When they are addressed, social skills are often taught in a resource room or other pullout program; however, it is also necessary to address these skills in mainstreamed settings and in less structured environments such as the lunchroom and the playground.

When working with learning-disabled students, it is important to consider the specific disabilities of the child. For example, students with more severe cognitive impairments may lack age-appropriate social understanding of complex interactions. Language-impaired students may have appropriate understanding of social situations but may have difficulty communicating effectively with others. Other students may have an adequate repertoire of problem-solving behaviors but lack the opportunity to practice them because of the self-contained nature of their educational program. Before implementing a social decision-making program, teachers can benefit from making a thorough evaluation of the strengths and weaknesses of each student. This will enable them to adapt the program to meet the needs of each child. It may also be advantageous to have heterogeneous groups when implementing social decision-making activities so that students can learn from each other.

The resource room or other pullout program (supplemental instruction, group counseling) has the advantage of working with a small group in a protected setting. This allows for a degree of intimacy and sharing not typically found in a larger class. In addition, because the resource room teacher provides a great deal of individual attention to each child, there may be a greater degree of trust and cohesion. It is important for the teacher to use this situation to good advantage while keeping in mind that the goal of the social decision-making program is to enable students to function independently outside the classroom.

Learning-disabled students derive many benefits when a regular time and place for social decision-making activities is established. Convey to students that this is a special part of the week during which you will help them develop social skills and solve everyday problems. Giving this time a specific name such as "sharing time" and having students form a circle can help to define it as different from their other educational activities.

FIG TESPN was initially developed as an alternative to presenting the problem-solving process as discrete steps because the learning-disabled students often have difficulty processing information in a sequential or linear manner. Some learning-disabled students, however, will have difficulty integrating all the parts of the process together. Teachers should therefore focus on both presenting FIG TESPN as a complete process *and* breaking down the process into discrete skills that can be taught individually. They can do this by repetition of the overall process during every lesson, focusing on one aspect for in-depth understanding and practice.

As with any other instructional material for learning-disabled students, it is helpful to use a multisensory approach. Some students will benefit from a verbal presentation and discussion; others require visual stimuli and cues; all students profit from actual practice of the skills through guided rehearsal in class and homework assignments to actually use the skills. Other ways to use a multisensory approach include having students make a videotape (some can write the script, direct, or act), draw cartoons depicting FIG TESPN helping them solve a problem, or cut out pictures from magazines reflecting different feelings. In addition, teachers can use popular television shows as a stimulus for discussion, with students developing and enacting alternate endings.

While written assignments involving social decision making can be helpful, this is often an aversive situation for learning-disabled students and should be kept to a minimum. Worksheets with guided questions requiring minimal written responses, as noted in Chapter 5, have been successful. Also, teacher-developed checklists can help students improve their decision-making and problem-solving vocabularies and reinforce the skills in a nonaversive manner. For example, the teacher can read a story and students can complete a worksheet such as the one that follows:

1. In the story, how was Tommy feeling when his friends went to the movies without him?

   Tommy was feeling: (circle how Tommy was feeling)

   sad   lonely   rejected   happy   bored   tired   content

2. Did Tommy have a problem? If so, what was it? (circle Tommy's problem)

   Tommy did not have a problem

   Tommy did not have any friends

   Tommy did not communicate to his friends what he wanted.

   Tommy's friends are mean.

3. What was Tommy's goal, what did he want to happen? etc.

THE GIFTED AND TALENTED

At one extreme in terms of cognitive ability, but not necessarily in terms of social awareness, are students with advanced abilities in some area of academic or creative talent. These students' social needs are often overlooked because their social sophistication is assumed to be commensurate with their intelligence. Obviously, this is not always the case.

When working with gifted students, teachers can point out the similarities between the social decision-making process and the scientific method. Gifted students of middle and high school age may not relate to FIG TESPN. If this is the case, FIG TESPN can be presented purely as a mnemonic rather than as a character that helps them problem solve. It can also be discussed as a process that students can apply to a variety of situations and problems.

Teachers may wish to present social decision making for gifted students by linking it first with academic applications. These students are likely to be more comfortable with an initial use of the approach in an academic setting. They can then see how the same kind of problem solving can be applied to social problems, as well.

When working on social decision-making activities, gifted students may have a better "feelings" vocabulary and can list a variety of feelings; this does not mean that they can adequately differentiate these feelings in themselves or others, however. An emphasis on awareness of feelings may help them explore new ways of knowing.

Gifted students typically are very good at brainstorming behavioral alternatives and anticipating consequences. But focusing on guided practice will be necessary to help them become comfortable actually using the skills. With all populations, it is necessary to conduct the discussion on a concrete level and have students practice solving problems, either through guided practice, live classroom experiences, or assignments. With the gifted, teachers must avoid assuming that a cognitive understanding and an ability to verbalize appropriate problem solving will guarantee spontaneous and appropriate exercise of the skills.

Other characteristics of gifted students sometimes overlooked because of their intelligence are their tendencies to be perfectionistic and, ironically, to have a low frustration tolerance despite their high level of ability. In such instances, they are likely to dwell on thoughts and feelings about their ability to succeed and the implications of not succeeding. This trait can interfere with many of their everyday activities and their willingness to challenge themselves socially or academically. Teachers can be alert to these students' negative self-statements and help them realistically sort out long- and short-term implications of their actions and possible outcomes. The use of FIG TESPN can help them envision a process of reaching their goals that may be rockier than many are used to, but that can be quite rewarding and growth-producing.

Finally, it may be useful to address specific types of problems that gifted students encounter, including—

- social rejection and teasing from peers
- difficulty relating to peers due to a lack of shared interests
- academic pressures
- difficulty reading subtle social cues
- "eccentric" behavior that contributes to social rejection.

In each of these instances, FIG TESPN, TVDRP, and many of the other worksheets and techniques given in this book can be used as the basis for individual and group problem solving.

STUDENTS WITH ATTENTION DEFICITS

Teachers who have worked with students who have attention deficits are aware of their deficits in social skills and their tendency to act impulsively rather than making thoughtful decisions. When working one-to-one, these students are often able to verbalize appropriate behaviors and are aware of consequences; but when in a group or away from adult supervision, they seem oblivious to rules and the repercussions of their actions. This can be frustrating to the teacher and disruptive to other students in the class. Ultimately, it is also frustrating to the student because of the inordinate amount of negative feedback he or she receives from others. Sadly, such students frequently find themselves in trouble, but unaware of how they got there.

Students with attention deficits need to focus on the self-control and group participation and social-awareness skills discussed in Chapter 3, especially Keep Calm. This skill needs to be prompted and practiced frequently. It is a prerequisite skill because if students do not first stop their activity and attend to what is going on around them, they will not be able to use the other, more complex, skills of social decision making and problem solving.

One way to help students inhibit their impulsivity is through self-verbalization. The use of this technique is implicit in FIG TESPN but it needs to be made explicit for students with attention deficits. Toward this end, the teacher should model the use of FIG TESPN frequently, having students verbalize the steps, as well as their responses. A fading procedure can be used whereby eventually the steps are whispered and then said silently by students. After all the steps have been taught and reinforced, the procedure can be shortened to emphasize defining the problem or decision, generating potential solutions, planning the implementation of the solution, and giving oneself feedback on the success with which plans are carried out. (Programs for teaching self-verbalization, such as Kendall's *Stop and Think Work Book*, are compatible with FIG TESPN and can be used as an adjunct. See Appendix B.)

Another helpful technique for students with attention deficits is training them to use their feelings as a cue to problem solving. These students tend to use feelings as a cue to engage in inappropriate behaviors—most typically, fight-or-flight reactions. The teacher will have opportunities in the classroom to be alert to situations that can engender negative emotional reactions in students and then help them use FIG TESPN before acting.

Assuming no other cognitive deficits, the student with an attention deficit can often use FIG TESPN one-on-one with an adult but have difficulty following up on plans that have been created. The teacher will need to break down the plan into small, clear units and monitor and reinforce each unit until the plan is carried out.

In general, students with attention deficits respond well to frequent monitoring and feedback on their behavior. Formal monitoring and reinforcement procedures (as used in behavior modification programs) can be applied to the use of social decision-making and problem-solving skills. For example, the teacher can make a chart for monitoring the use of Keep Calm and FIG TESPN. Each successful prompted use earns one point; each spontaneous use earns two points. Five points entitles the student to a specific reward such as free time. Teachers may also wish to include students' self-reports of use of a social decision-making technique, even though they cannot verify them. However, such reports encourage students at least to think of times outside the classroom when they might have used the technique and to articulate it clearly to their teachers.

EMOTIONALLY DISTURBED (ED) POPULATIONS

ED populations are among the most challenging and most needy in terms of teaching social skills. With such students, it is important to differentiate between those with a skill deficit and those with a performance deficit. Students with a skill deficit have not mastered the basic social skills necessary to engage appropriately with others or to solve social problems. Students with a performance deficit have the skills but do not use them, due to a lack of intrinsic or extrinsic motivators. The former group needs an emphasis on skill development; for the latter group, it is necessary to identify the factors that serve to motivate or inhibit performance of the skills and help these students understand such factors. It may also be necessary to establish tangible motivators in programs for elementary and middle school students—i.e., the consequences for inappropriate social behaviors are aversive and the consequences for prosocial behaviors and the use of social decision making are desirable. The skills checklist (see Table 2–1 in Chapter 2) can help teachers differentiate between skill and performance deficits.

With an ED population, obviously, other issues also interfere in social development. However, social skills promotion can help these students break out of maladaptive behavior patterns and begin to feel more capable. Because they can assume that regardless of their behaviors the outcomes will be negative, it is important to provide these students with small, tangible successes. By seeing that appropriate social skills enable them to have their needs met, they can begin to experience the naturally reinforcing consequences of appropriate social behavior.

It is also necessary to "inoculate" these fragile students against further experiences of failure and rejection. In the planning phase of FIG TESPN, it is essential to anticipate potential obstacles to implementing their plans and achieving their goals. Once these obstacles have been identified, second-order FIG TESPNs can be carried out to decide how to overcome them. Also, the student must be taught to use self-coping statements when confronted with challenges. The last FIG TESPN step can be extended to include the teaching of and prompting for self-coping statements (e.g., "I can do it." "I am capable." "Effort is what counts and I'm trying hard.").

POPULATIONS OF DIFFERENCE

With increasingly pluralistic, multicultural, and ethnically diverse school populations, educators will constantly face students who are different from the majority group in their classrooms, school, and/or communities. Rather than addressing every other subpopulation that teachers might find themselves working with, this section provides a general discussion on how to adapt the program to meet the needs of any "population of difference." By using the following guidelines and focusing on the concepts of differentness, strengths, and respect for diversity, a social decision-making program can be adapted to such diverse populations as ethnic minorities, children of poverty, children of alcoholics, children of divorce, and underachievers.

1. *Identify the strengths* of the population and use these strengths to bolster self-esteem and compensate for areas of weakness. For example, students who have experienced stress due to family or environmental problems can discuss how they have successfully coped with these problems in the past. These successful problem-solving examples can be put into the FIG TESPN framework. Some students may have strengths in sensitivity toward feelings because of their experiences, although they might not be dealing with these feelings appropriately.
2. *Identify specific needs* of the population in terms of knowledge, skill, or attitude. For example, in a program for teenage pregnancy prevention, it will be necessary to inform students about what is involved in raising a child so that they will be able to more accurately "envision the end results." Some populations will need more skill development than others in effective communication skills. Additional lessons can be developed around these needs.
3. *Review the readiness skills and FIG TESPN* and identify those skills that may be most readily mastered and those that may be most difficult. This will give the teacher an indication of the pace at which to work. Each lesson can last one session or continue through several lessons. Also, lessons can be repeated or extended. Repetition is necessary for mastery. The overall age and cognitive development level of students will also influence the pace and concreteness of the lessons.
4. *Be sensitive to the differences* of these students in terms of perspective and social norms. Cultural and social factors influence the goals and potential solutions that will be generated. Regardless of the population the teacher is working with, it is necessary to suspend critical judgment of anything proposed by the student. For example, children of alcoholics are likely to have witnessed some extraordinary negative behavior. As a result, many of their standards for solving problems,

handling stress, and relating to others will be distorted. They will need patience and supportive assistance as they gradually work through their very strong feelings, clarify goals, and learn to make socially appropriate, realistic plans. The teacher's role of facilitating thinking through the problem so that these students can make better decisions becomes essential for their long-term growth. If the teacher censors certain goals or options, this puts her/him in an authority role, inhibits students' ability to think through the consequences of their actions, and helps trap students in maladaptive problem-solving and decision-making strategies.

5. *Review the steps in FIG TESPN* and identify those that may be most important to the population. Emphasize those steps through extended discussion or lessons. For example, for students with a substance abuse problem, it is important to focus on their goals. What do they want out of life? Where would they like to be in five years? Then, focus on end results. If they continue to use drugs, where do they picture themselves in five days? five weeks? five months? five years? With children of divorce, extra attention to clarifying feelings is important. For members of ethnic and cultural minorities, feelings and goals are important, but so is an ability to look at alternatives and make realistic, workable plans.

6. *Identify typical problems* students face and tailor instruction to those problems. Teachers may first wish to use more general, less threatening examples and then move to more personal and relevant ones. Stories that provide analogous situations are useful, as is TVDRP.

SUMMARY

Above all, when tailoring the program to subgroups, it is necessary for the teacher to listen carefully to students. Through receiving active listening, students will feel their experiences validated and accepted. In addition, the teacher can then begin to identify the specific circumstances, strengths, and needs of students. Through listening, teachers can become focused on their students' sensitivities and adapt social decision-making lessons and activities to fit their students' needs.

7. CONCLUSIONS . . . AND BEGINNINGS

There are times when we cannot let other people do our thinking for us; we must think for ourselves. And we must learn to think for ourselves.... The point is that students must be encouraged to become reasonable for their own good (i.e., as a step toward their own autonomy) and not just for our good (i.e., because the growing rationalization of the society requires it). (51, p. 43)

There is always a gap between reading about new curriculum and instruction procedures and putting them into action. In the field of education and in other fields that study the spread of innovations into existing systems, that gap can sometimes widen into an insurmountable chasm. Certain things can be done, however, to ensure that the gap remains small and eventually disappears. This chapter cannot cover in detail all the procedures for bringing new curriculum and instruction procedures into practice. Much has been written in that area, including quite a bit that relates specifically to programs in the social and affective domain (5, 30, 31, 41, 67, 74). This chapter provides elements that we have found useful in turning educators' initial enthusiasm into the kinds of beginning action that can result in making the social decision-making approach a part of the everyday routine.

BASIC PRINCIPLES

Start small. The history of change—both large-scale and classroom-size—shows that change begins with a small pilot effort. This is equally true for lasting, meaningful change in curriculum and instruction procedures. Select some aspect of what you have read in the preceding chapters and set up a pilot project in which you begin to apply the ideas and monitor their effectiveness. Set very modest goals; do not begin a program by expecting it to solve your most difficult classroom or behavioral problems. The history of change shows that successful program development takes from three to five years. The pilot year provides the implementer with a basic idea of how the procedure works. It is a significant step from reading about it to putting it into practice.

After the first-year pilot activities, the implementer is in a much better position to think about how the program works and how it can apply to his or her particular concerns. Further, by its very nature, a pilot year should contain many different types of attempts. For example, you might use social decision making by attempting to work with one or two self-control and social awareness skills. Or you might begin by applying FIG TESPN to social studies or language arts. Or perhaps you might institute a weekly half-hour period for group sharing and discussion, and proceed using the type of framework outlined in Chapters 3 and 4. The point is that in the first year, you should try several different strategies to see their "fit." The analogy of shopping in a marvelous clothing store and taking the time to try on different outfits is appropriate here.

Similar to shopping for clothes, you will find that you begin to narrow down the strategies to those that are most comfortable for you to use. And, once again like the clothing store, you may choose one or many strategies, depending on your situation. Indeed, seasons change. Applications of social decision making that are successful at a particular time with a particular grade level or student population may evolve as you continue to work with that population. Or they may shift radically as you encounter a new "season." The second year, therefore, is devoted to selecting those strategies that you are most pleased with, putting them into your repertoire throughout the entire year, and then seeing how they affect your work.

The first year, then, is for familiarization; the second year is for teachers to learn well what they are attempting to do. In the third year, most often referred to as the consolidation year (30), teachers master the instructional procedures to the point that they are prepared to use them most effectively. And students become the beneficiaries.

Be prepared to change your role. A new program is not a simple set of activities. It requires integration into a view of one's role in the schools. The social decision-making approach is aligned with several different kinds of roles. When using this approach, educators become significant sources of support, by providing a positive, caring, safe, predictable learning environment. By focusing on self-control and social awareness, educators make it clear that there is a structure and a set of limits that will be respected, and part of those things are the feelings and rights of other people. Another role is that of facilitator of others' thinking through the use of FIG TESPN and facilitative questioning and modeling techniques. Instructors let it be known that they value students' thoughtfulness. They convey the fact that their role is not to solve students' problems but to help *give them the skills* to solve their problems. Along with this role is an expectation that students can solve their problems, which is a great motivator and encourager, particularly for students with learning difficulties or a history of disengagement from the school.

An additional role is that of prompter of self-control and social awareness. Through social decision-making approaches, the instructor conveys that students are not expected to sit in a classroom, hear concepts, and put them into practice immediately. There is an implicit, shared responsibility for learning. Teachers provide concepts, and then seek to help students understand their appropriate use by prompting the use of the relevant skills as needed. Finally, the teacher takes on the role of provider of thinking frameworks. Many of the activities in Chapters 3, 4, and 5 are alternative ways of building students' thoughtful social decision making and problem solving. These frameworks are applied to social studies, to monitoring individual progress, to behavioral interactions with peers, and to a variety of other areas. They serve as roadmaps for students on the ultimate road to academic and social success and health. These variations in role pervade the teacher's interactions with students, extending well beyond the specific instructional time in which new procedures are being used. It is for this reason that we emphasize the importance of classroom teachers carrying out social decision-making activities, rather than having such activities conveyed primarily through pullout programs or by professionals who come into the classroom on a weekly basis to work with students.

Seek support. In the beginning, it is very helpful for teachers to use a set of procedures to share what they are doing with other people. This can be as small scale as sharing information about their efforts with the principal, the school psychologist, the social worker, the learning specialist, the guidance counselor, the instructional supervisor, or a neighboring teacher. Ideally, the teacher will generate sufficient interest so that a colleague will be willing to observe and become a "partner" during the learning phase. Indeed, it is very helpful if a colleague observes as the teacher carries out the social decision-making approach in the early stages of learning.

A useful format for gaining support over a long period of time is through group supervision. The purpose of such supervision is for teachers and other school-based professionals to provide mutual support and guidance to one another. It is based on the premise that a structured and regular avenue for discussion will further increase knowledge and skills.

The goals of group supervision are as follows:

1. to assist teachers in planning their social problem-solving (SPS) lessons
2. to assist teachers in working through individual problems with the SPS curriculum
3. to assist teachers in working with individual students who are experiencing problems in social and/or academic areas
4. to build a library of supplementary curriculum materials
5. to further adapt and develop the entire SPS curriculum.

Group supervision assumes a certain level of knowledge and skill. Before beginning, it would be helpful for all teachers to be familiar with this publication or some other common source of instructional information. In addition, they should be prepared to work on social decision making on a regular and frequent basis with their students. A set of formal lesson plans is helpful but not essential; however, it is necessary that teachers document their lesson in some manner.

Group meetings on a regular and relatively frequent basis are important. The meeting schedule should be established in the beginning of the year.

At the beginning of each session, an agenda should be developed. We have found the following framework to be useful:

- Reviewing SPS lessons taught and problems/successes encountered
- Sharing sample materials, lessons, and worksheets developed by individual teachers (copies for all participants should be brought)
- Brainstorming and initial outlining of additional lessons designed to meet specific classroom needs
- Discussing individual problems—either in terms of lessons or students.

During the group supervision, it is important to stay on topic and proceed in an organized manner. While some informal information exchange may be helpful, it should be kept at a minimum. A certain amount of time can be allotted to this on the agenda. Although group supervision is leaderless, there should be a rotating facilitator whose responsibility is to keep the discussion on topic, to coordinate any additional actions that are planned during the meeting, and to see to the logistics for the meetings (time, space, refreshments, materials).

The last few group supervision meetings of the school year should be dedicated to an evaluation of the year's social decision-making and problem-solving activities. The evaluation should include curriculum and related activities, how they were implemented, and the group supervision process. Group members may wish to come to these meetings with the following:

- the best lessons and why
- the worst lessons and why
- implementation successes
- implementation failures
- rating 1 (poor) to 5 (good) of the group supervision with suggestions for improvement.

The group supervision process can then be used to plan the following year's social decision-making activities and their implementation.

Despite group supervision, or when such supervision is not feasible, there will be times when it is useful to tap some external experience and expertise in social decision-making instruction. Having recognized this issue throughout the course of our work, we have developed several "antidotes for isolation." One antidote is to provide a regular set of training experiences, based at a continuing education center at Rutgers University and the University of Medicine and Dentistry of New Jersey-Community Mental Health Center (UMDNJ-CMHC) at Piscataway. These training experiences, attended by people from all over the country, lead to networks of ongoing contacts, which are sustained through various needs:

- The social decision-making approach has been approved by the Program Effectiveness Panel of the National Diffusion Network (NDN) and our project is a developer/demonstrator project of that network. Therefore, a network of public school and private school facilitators in each state can be accessed through the NDN. These individuals can serve as a contact and method of making liaison both with the main project program sites in New Jersey and with other neighboring districts in which social decision-making activities are being conducted.

- *The Problem Solving Connection Newsletter,* published jointly by Rutgers University and the UMDNJ-CMHC at Piscataway, is sent two or three times each year to hundreds of educators in the United States, the United Kingdom, Australia, and Canada, who are interested in or are actively using the social decision-making approach. The newsletter is designed as a resource exchange. People ask questions about instructional or program-related problems they are having and the newsletter offices provide answers from various readers. Previous issues of the newsletter serve as a compendium of ideas and techniques that people have used to adapt social decision making to a variety of populations and instructional circumstances. In other words, the PSC is a vehicle for having contact with a community of educators and other professionals using the social decision-making approach, and a means for not having to "reinvent the wheel."

- The UMDNJ-CMHC at Piscataway has a service delivery unit called the Social Problem Solving Program. As part of this service delivery unit, the CMHC has set up a toll-free telephone number (1–800–245–7702 or 7762). Teachers can call in questions for the PSC or have their questions responded to by a consultant or by the faxing of existing materials and documents with which the caller might not be familiar.

- *Reach out to parents.* A social decision-making program is enriched by finding meaningful roles for parents. This is as true at the high school level as it is at the elementary or middle-school level. However, it is recognized that the earlier parents find roles in this (or any) element of schooling, the more likely they are to sustain those roles.

    Parents can be engaged in a social decision-making program at three levels: they can be informed, involved, or included.

- *Informing parents* means letting them know what is going on in the classroom. This can take place at back-to-school nights or special parent meetings by describing the program or, most effectively, by running groups of parents though simulated lessons. Several meetings over the course of the year can be held, corresponding to different phases of social decision-making instruction.

- *Involving parents* means seeking their active support of the school-based learning and/or its home extensions. This can take place through meetings and also through what our colleague Charlotte Hett calls "refrigerator notes." These one-page handouts summarize a concept taught in class (e.g., Classroom Constitution, Keep Calm, FIG TESPN) and make concrete suggestions to parents about how to recognize and reinforce the use of the skill by the child, use prompts and cues to elicit the skill in trigger situations, and/or apply the skill to commonly recurring home situations and routines.

- *Including parents* means giving them the skills to creatively integrate social decision making into their home routines and parenting practices. This can be done by having them read relevant resource materials (see Appendix B), or by holding four-to-six-session group meetings, co-led by teachers and/or school psychologists, social workers, guidance counselors, or health educators. A useful framework for such sessions is to have group members read specific material and discuss uses of the ideas and methods with children from preschool through high school as relevant to a particular group; as ways parents can use the skills to relieve their own life stress; and as applications to such topics as homework, discipline, peer relationships, and college and career choices. Parenting centers can be developed and staffed, at least in part, by parents to gather and provide parenting information, using methods similar to those suggested for group supervision to compile parent questions and suggested solutions to problems. (Much relevant information has already been gathered as part of a continuing series called *Parenting Matters*. See Appendix B for further information on obtaining parent-related resources.)

CONCLUSIONS . . . BEGINNINGS

This book is intended to provide a brief but practical introduction to a most exciting and relevant area of curriculum and instruction in the schools. It contains enough information to allow educators to start small, to begin to change their role, and to gain support and skill in the instructional methods outlined. We and others using social decision making firmly believe that this approach makes a significant contribution to education by making a significant contribution to the way students think and interact with peers and adults. We invite readers to consult the followup resources in Appendix B for additional information. Many of the techniques described in this book are complementary to others with which readers are no doubt familiar. We encourage the creative integration of FIG TESPN and the remainder of the social decision-making framework into those strategies that are already being implemented for the benefit of students.

APPENDIXES

A. SAMPLE STORIES FOR STUDENTS

Think Now for Later: Keeping Your Body in Shape
by Maurice J. Elias

Every day, each of us makes many decisions that affect our health. We choose what to eat, when to eat, and how much to eat. We decide when and how to keep our bodies clean. We think about the air we breathe and try to keep it clean. And we all know what happens if we are not careful with our decisions. Just think about a time you've eaten too much, or you've eaten too late at night. What a lousy feeling in your stomach and your whole body! And when you haven't kept clean, you probably remember how your hair might have felt itchy and greasy. You didn't look your best and maybe your skin even got worse. Everybody knows how awful it is when the air isn't clean. Just think about how horrible it is when you drive past the oil refineries on the turnpike or when you come into a room filled with cigarette smoke or, even more upsetting, cigar smoke.

Being healthy and living in a healthy world does, as we said in the beginning, involve *decisions* and *choices*. What exactly *is* a "decision"? What exactly is a "choice"? Go look up these words in a dictionary and write the meanings either in the spaces below or on your answer sheet.

decision: _____

_____

_____

choice: _____

_____

_____

_____

As you found out, both decisions and choices involve *thinking*, thinking about what you want to have happen and different ways of getting things to happen. To make a good, healthy decision, you have to know what your *goals* are. Bad decisions—decisions that will make you less healthy, make you less alert, and make your body less able to do what you want it to—are usually made because people are not sure what their goals are. They aren't thinking about *the future*. They aren't *thinking now for later*.

Bad decisions are decisions that end up harming your body or your mind. They make you *less* healthy, not more healthy. Smoking, taking drugs, abusing alcohol—these are not things that "everybody" does. These things happen to people who make *bad decisions*, who don't think now for later.

Nobody will ever tell you it's smart to smoke, take drugs, or abuse alcohol. Nobody does it because it's smart.

Nobody ever smokes, takes drugs, or drinks to impress parents or

114

teachers. Nobody does it because they think adults who care about them will be proud of them.

So why do people smoke or use smokeless tobacco or take drugs or abuse alcohol? Because they have made *bad decisions*. They didn't *think now for later*. Most of them will never admit it, even if you ask them. Many people are afraid to say, "I made a bad decision." It doesn't mean they are bad people. But it does mean they made a bad decision and until they stop what they are doing and make new choices, they are harming their bodies or their minds or *both*.

And people who make bad decisions about their health are *ashamed*. So what do they do? Right! *They try to make their bad decision sound good!* And they try to get others to do what they do. Because if you drink or smoke too, then you won't be able to say anything to them. Deep down, you'll feel ashamed, your body will feel different, and your mind will not be the same. People don't like to admit this kind of stuff, so instead, they make it all sound cool and nice and wonderful. But if you *think now for later*, you will decide how this will affect your body and your mind—your *only* body and your *only* mind.

When you *think now for later*, you ask yourself, "Is this going to hurt me, make me weak or sick or less alert?" If the answer is yes, you should *decide not to do it*. And if you're not sure, do you think it's a good decision to try it and see? Or would a better decision be to learn more, to find out more from someone who *knows* and who is *not* doing it? Remember, if you think now for later—TNFL—you'll make better decisions and better choices and be a healthier, more alert person!

THINK NOW FOR LATER: WHAT CAN HAPPEN IF YOU DON'T AND IF YOU DO

We stay healthy because we make decisions and choices that do not harm our bodies or our minds. Sure, it's easy to skip a shower or not bother to brush our teeth. It may seem easy to say "yes" when someone offers you a cigarette or a beer. But if we *think now for later*, we will make better, healthier decisions. After all, who loses if we spend our afternoons in a dentist's chair or ruin our lungs?—we do!

Let's take a look at some children your age who are in the middle of making important decisions and choices about their health. As you read, ask yourself how you might feel if you were Charlie or Warren. Which of them is *thinking now for later*?

Going Down the Tobacco Road . . . or the Healthy Road?

Warren and Charlie were watching television at Charlie's house. They were getting ready for Monday at West End Middle School. They had watched for most of the day, since it was too rainy to do much outside.

Warren was watching a commercial for smokeless tobacco. "Boy," he said to himself, "that guy is really cool. And it looks so easy. You just stick it in your lip, and wow, you'd probably feel great. I'd like to look just like that guy on TV. Even on television, some of those cool cops and other guys have been doing smokeless tobacco instead of smoking. Maybe I'll stop smoking and get some of that tobacco stuff."

Charlie was watching the same thing, but had some different thoughts. "Wow," he said to himself, "that guy looks pretty cool. And it sure sounds easy to do. But I wonder what that stuff can do to your lip and mouth? I read somewhere that some of the stuff in tobacco is the same stuff that makes cigarettes give you cancer. Can you imagine having cancer in your mouth? All the sores and everything . . . how could you eat pizza and ice cream and donuts? Smoking may hurt you, but that smokeless tobacco stuff seems just as dumb to me. There are smarter ways to be cool."

At school the next day, Warren saw Charlie. "Hey Charlie, you wanna try some of this smokeless stuff? I saw it on TV and it looked really great." "No thanks, Warren. I don't want sores and junk in my mouth." "But didn't you see that guy on TV? He said it was easy." "Yeah, but he didn't say what would happen after a while. I bet he just uses it during commercials."

Warren and Charlie watched the same commercial but thought about it very differently. Charlie is worried about his health—he's *thinking now for later*. What is Warren thinking about? His goal is to be cool, to feel "great," or to do what's "easy." It's not bad to be "cool," but when the choice is between being cool or being healthy, it's important to *think now for later*. There are other ways to be cool or feel great, without cigarettes or smokeless tobacco. Charlie chooses the road to health, and keeps his mouth from getting sores, and maybe cancer, later on.

Let's meet two girls your age who are trying to do their school work but have different ideas about what to do when the work gets hard, or just boring. As you read, think about Janet, Carol, and Katie and whom you know in your school who is like each of them.

Pills for Thrills . . . or Poison for Your Body?

Carol was over at Janet's house. They were studying together for a test in Social Studies, and then they were going to work on a book report for English. They had been working for an hour or so, when Carol started to get restless. "This is boring," Carol said. "I can't stand this." Carol got up and went into the bathroom. She came out after a couple of minutes and showed a bottle of pills to Janet. "Do you want one?" "What's that?" "Oh, these are some pills I take when I get bored or down or sad. I got them from Katie, you know, that ninth grader who hangs around when we get out of middle school." "Her? Boy, I wouldn't even trust her to give me a pretzel. Did you ever take a good look at her?" Carol stopped to think. "No, I never have," she said. "Well, you should. She's all skinny and wasted and she looks like she hasn't slept in a month. What a wreck!"

All of a sudden, they heard a key in the door—Janet's parents were back. Carol rushed to put the pills in her book bag. Janet was really surprised at the panic-stricken look on Carol's face. "Carol, you looked so scared."

116

"Yeah, well, these pills are illegal—you can get in trouble if you get caught with them." "Why?" asked Janet. "I don't know," Carol said, "Maybe you should have a prescription or something." Janet said, "Well, then how do you know what's in it, or where it comes from, or how much to take?" Carol was getting annoyed. She said, "Katie told me it was okay. Besides, I get to go to her house and see her friends and listen to her stereo tapes and use her headphones. You ought to come!"

Janet thought for a minute. Katie seemed like a loser. And those pills could be really dangerous. Real medicine is made carefully, in clean places, and with doses that a doctor says are right for you. These pills are, well, very risky . . . *too* risky, thought Janet. But Katie had older friends, a great stereo, and some parties that were really wild. It might be exciting to be her friend . . .

Janet finally answered, "No, I don't think so. It wouldn't be worth hurting myself, maybe really badly, just to be Katie's friend or go to her house. She's no friend if she tries to get you to take pills."

Janet faced some hard choices. What were all the reasons for her to try the pills? When Janet's parents came home, what happened? Was Carol proud of what she did or was she ashamed and scared? Would you choose seeing older kids and using a good stereo if it meant losing your health? Was Carol *thinking now for later?*

When Carol said to Janet, "Do you want one?" she was really asking, "DO YOU WANT TO POISON YOUR BODY?" And we know this is true, because we know about Katie. Janet noticed how Katie looked—awful. Carol never let herself see what pills had done to Katie—and what they would do to her or *anyone* who tries them. Carol didn't *think now for later*. Sure, there might be some fun hours with Katie and her cool friends—but the clock would strike midnight, and the magic spell would be broken. Carol would have to come back to reality. And if she became addicted to pills—then, the road back to health would be harder. Janet would always remember:

When anyone asks you to try pills, drugs, or alcohol . . .
They are really asking, "DO YOU WANT TO POISON YOUR BODY?"
If you say Yes to be cool, you may end up as a fool.
If you say Yes to feel great, you'll end up with a sad fate.

Finally, we're going to meet Robert and Connie. Both have health problems that require visits to the doctor pretty often. They also have to take medication and do special treatments This is true for many youngsters, such as those with asthma, allergies, diabetes, and, in a similar way, for youngsters with problems that are mostly physical. Having to take care of yourself so carefully can be a pain. But it's also a *choice*, a *decision about your health*. Let's see what Robert and Connie are feeling and thinking, as they get ready for yet *another* visit to the doctor.

Not Following Doctor's Orders: Putting One Over . . . or Putting Yourself Under?

When Robert walked into the doctor's office, he was surprised to see Connie in the waiting room. Robert and Connie were classmates at Campbell Middle School. They were both at the doctor's for checkups. Robert has asthma and Connie has allergies. They both had to take medications and do certain breathing exercises. And they both didn't like to do these things.

"Hi, Connie. Isn't this a real drag? My parents drag me here every two weeks. I really hate it!" "So do I. Every morning they bother me to take the medicine, take the medicine, take the medicine. Sometimes I just pretend to take it, and then I throw it out." Robert looked surprised. "You do? Why?" Connie said, "They hassle me so much that I've got to do *something*. So, I show them. I put those tablets in my cheek and spit them out in the bathroom."

Robert thought about what Connie said. He also hated the medicine, the doctor's visits, and the breathing machine. But he never thought about doing what Connie did. Sure, he got upset at his parents for always reminding him. But what if he didn't take the medicine? He'd probably feel the same for a little while, but after a few days—big trouble! It didn't make any sense to hurt himself just because he was angry at his parents.

"Connie, I don't understand why you pretend with the pills. It just hurts you!" "But I've *got* to do *something*. I didn't ask to be sick, and at least I can show my parents that I have some choices that are mine." "Connie, that doesn't make any sense. If you want to show you can do stuff, show it in some other way, maybe with your writing or your music or something else. You're good at *those* things. It just seems weird to take a chance on making yourself sicker when you're upset about being sick! You'll end up with more medicines and treatments!"

Now it was Connie's turn to do a little thinking.

If you were Connie, what would you be thinking? Perhaps you'd say to yourself, "I definitely have a problem. I hate these medicines. I hate being sick. And I hate everybody telling me what to do and how to do it. Well, I *do* have allergies and I can't wish them away. And when I get an attack, wow, it sure is painful. Once they even thought I'd die! What do I want most that I can have?"

Connie's answer would probably be to show her parents, and others, that there is a lot she *can* do. But if she doesn't take her medicine, how would that help? If her parents found out—and they probably would, when she had an attack—they might ground her. And they *certainly* wouldn't trust her. If you were Connie, it would probably be a good idea to *think now for later*. Do what has to be done to *stay healthy*. Your parents will trust you and you will feel as well as *you* can feel. Then, you can think of different ways of showing what you can do, or how you feel. Robert had two good suggestions for Connie: through writing or music. It's natural to get angry at doctors or your parents or medicine or treatments. But if you *think now for later*, you'll remember how things would be *without* medicine and treatment. By putting one over on the doctors, you may really be putting yourself under.

Wrapping It Up: It's Your Body and Your Mind

There are many important decisions and choices that we have to make about our health. Sometimes, our friends or people we know will make suggestions that may seem good at the time. But if we *think now for later*, we might realize that we can poison our body or poison our mind if we follow their ideas. It can be hard to say, "No," to resist these ideas. What will your friends think? Will they reject you or tease you? Charlie, Janet, and Robert thought and made decisions that will be good for their health. It wasn't easy, but they told their friends they wouldn't follow along, that it is more important to be healthy than to be "cool" or try to show adults that you can put one over on them. You have one body and one mind—if you choose *now* to keep them both healthy, you'll have them in good working condition for lots of fun things *later*.

B. RESOURCES FOR TEACHERS

Curriculum Resources for Social Decision-Making Instruction

1. *Social Decision Making Skills: A Curriculum Guide for the Elementary Grades,* by Maurice J. Elias and John F. Clabby (1989)

   Aspen Publishers, 1600 Research Boulevard, Rockville, MD 20850 (1–800–638–8437)

2. *FIG TESPN Goes to Middle School: A Three Year Social Decision Making and Problem Solving Curriculum for Middle School Special Education Students,* by Steven Tobias and Maurice J. Elias (1989)

   Professional Center at Somerset, Suite 103, 11 Clyde Road, Somerset, NJ 08873

3. *Readiness Lessons for Social Decision Making: Middle School Level,* by Charlotte Hett, Howard Rubenstein, and the Improving Social Awareness-Social Problem Solving Team (1989)

   UMDNJ–CMHC at Piscataway, 240 Stelton Road, Piscataway, NJ 08854–3248

4. *The Yale-New Haven Social Development Curriculum—Secondary Level,* by Roger P. Weissberg (1989)

   Yale University, Department of Psychology, Box 11A Yale Station, New Haven, CT 06520

5. *Interpersonal Cognitive Problem Solving Curriculum for Preschool and Kindergarten,* by Myrna Shure and George Spivack (1974)

   Jossey-Bass Publishers, 350 Sansome Street, San Francisco, CA 94104

6. *Stop and Think Workbook,* by Philip C. Kendall (1988)

   238 Meeting House Lane, Merion Station, PA 19066

7. *Picture Arrangement Story Telling,* by Steven Tobias, Brian Friedlander, and Maurice J. Elias (1990)

   Professional Center at Somerset, Suite 103, 11 Clyde Road, Somerset, NJ 08873

Resources for Obtaining Video Materials

1. *Agency for Instructional Technology*
   Catalogue of Materials—1989
   Box A, Bloomington, IN 47402
   1–800–457–4509

2. *Public Television Stations*
   Contact local stations for broadcast schedules and information about dubbing or taping off the air.

3. *Audiovisual Libraries*
   Many counties, education resource centers, and college and university libraries maintain audiovisual catalogues and libraries from which videos, films, and audiotapes may be borrowed and/or copied.

4. *Center for Research on the Influence of Television on Children (CRITC)*
   John C. Wright and Aletha C. Huston, Co-Directors
   Department of Human Development, University of Kansas, Lawrence, KS 66045–2133

Resources for Working with Parents Using the Social Decision-Making Approach

1. *Teach Your Child Decision Making* (paperback edition), by John F. Clabby and Maurice J. Elias (1986)

   Doubleday and Co., Publisher. Distributed by the authors.

2. *Parenting Matters: A Continuing Series of Applications of Social Decision Making to Everyday Parenting Issues,* by Maurice J. Elias (ongoing)

   Maurice J. Elias, c/o *The Home News,* P.O. Box 551, 123 How Lane, New Brunswick, NJ 08903–0551

3. *Problem-Solving Techniques in Childrearing,* by Myrna Shure and George Spivack (1978)

   Jossey-Bass Publishers, 350 Sansome Street, San Francisco, CA 94104

Resources for Training and Ongoing Support of Social Decision-Making Instruction

1. *Continuing Education Center for Social Competence Promotion, Social Decision Making and Prevention*
   Rutgers University and University of Medicine and Dentistry of New Jersey-Community Mental Health Center at Piscataway
   Co-Directors: Maurice J. Elias and John F. Clabby
   Administrator: Thomas Schuyler
   Coordinator of Professional Development: Linda Bruene
   Write c/o Director, Center for Applied Psychology, Graduate School of Applied and Professional Psychology, Rutgers University, Busch Campus, Piscataway, NJ 08854.

2. *Social Problem-Solving Training Program*
   John Clabby, Director
   UMDNJ-CMHC at Piscataway
   240 Stelton Road
   Piscataway, NJ 08854–3248
   FAX No. 201–463–5115
   1–800–245–7702 or 7762

3. *Problem Solving Connection Newsletter*
   Charlotte Hett, Managing Editor
   UMDNJ-CMHC at Piscataway
   240 Stelton Road
   Piscataway, NJ 08854–3248

4. *National Diffusion Network (NDN)*
   Write to the NDN at U.S. Department of Education, 555 New Jersey
   Avenue, NW, Washington, DC 20208–1525 or call (202) 357–6134 to find
   out how to contact NDN facilitators in your state.

Resources for Research Related to Social Decision Making

1. *Improving Social Awareness-Social Problem Solving Project.*
   Maurice J. Elias, Research Director
   Rutgers University, Department of Psychology, Tillett Hall, Livingston
   Campus, New Brunswick, NJ 08903
   FAX No. 201–932–2263

2. *Yale-New Haven Social Problem Solving Project*
   Roger P. Weissberg, Research Director
   Yale University, Department of Psychology, Box 11A Yale Station, New
   Haven, CT 06520
   FAX No. 203–432–7172

3. *Rochester Primary Mental Health Project*
   Emory Cowen, Research Director
   Center for Community Study, 575 Mt. Hope Avenue, Rochester, NY 14623

4. *Interpersonal Cognitive Problem Solving Project*
   George Spivack, Research Director
   Institute for Graduate and Clinical Psychology, Widener University,
   Chester, PA 19013

GLOSSARY OF ACRONYMS

BEST. *B*ody posture, *E*ye contact, Things to *s*ay, and *T*one of voice.

FIG TESPN. An acronym for the sequence of steps that guide students through the process of social decision making and problem solving (see Table 4–1).

ISA. Improving Social Awareness.

ISA-SPS. Improving Social Awareness/Social Problem Solving Project.

NAPSEC. National Association of Private Schools for Exceptional Children.

NDN. National Diffusion Network (of the U.S. Department of Education).

PSC. Problem Solving Connection (newsletter).

SPS. Social problem solving.

TNFL. Think Now for Later.

TVDRP. Television-Based Discussion and Guided Rehearsal and Practice.

UMDNJ–CMHC. University of Medicine and Dentistry of New Jersey-Community Mental Health Center.

VENT. *V*oice tone, *E*ye contact, *N*ice language, and *T*all posture.

BIBLIOGRAPHY

1. Agency for Instructional Technology. *Catalogue of Instructional Materials.* Bloomington, Ind.: AIT, 1989.
2. Alexander, F., and Crabtree, C. "California's New History-Social Science Curriculum Promises Richness and Depth." *Educational Leadership* 46 (1988): 10–13.
3. Asarnow, J.; Carlson, G.; and Guthrie, D. "Coping Strategies, Self-perceptions, Hopelessness, and Perceived Family Environments in Depressed and Suicidal Children." *Journal of Consulting and Clinical Psychology* 55 (1987): 361–66.
4. Baron, J., and Brown, R., eds. *Adolescent Decision Making.* Hillsdale, N.J.: Erlbaum, in press.
5. Basch, C. E. "Research on Disseminating and Implementing Health Education Programs in the Schools." *Journal of School Health* 54 (1983): 57–66.
6. Bernard, B.; Fafoglia, G.; and Perone, J. "Knowing What to Do—and Not to Do—Reinvigorates Drug Education." *Association for Supervision and Curriculum Development Curriculum Update*, February 1987, 1–12.
7. Botvin, G. J. "Prevention of Substance Abuse Through the Development of Personal and Social Competence." In *Preventing Adolescent Drug Abuse: Intervention Strategies*, edited by T. Glynn, C. Leukefeld, and J. Ludford. NIDA Research Monograph #47. Rockville, Md.: National Institute of Drug Abuse, 1983.
8. _____. "The Life Skills Training Program as a Health Promotion Strategy: Theoretical Issues and Empirical Findings." In *Health Promotion in the Schools*, edited by J. Zins, D. Wagner, and C. Maher, pp. 9–23. New York: Haworth, 1985.
9. Bransford, J.; Sherwood, R.; Vye, N.; and Rieser, J. "Teaching Thinking and Problem Solving: Research Foundations." *American Psychologist* 41 (1986): 1078–89.
10. Bronfenbrenner, U. "Contexts of Child Rearing: Problems and Prospects." *American Psychologist* 34 (1979): 844–50.
11. Brophy, J. "Teacher Influences on Student Achievement." *American Psychologist* 41 (1986): 1069–77.
12. Bryant, J., and Anderson, D., eds. *Children's Understanding of Television: Research on Attention and Comprehension.* New York: Academic Press, 1983.
13. Cangelosi, J. *Cooperation in the Classroom: Students and Teachers Together.* 2d ed. Washington, D.C.: National Education Association, 1990.
14. Cartledge, G., and Milburn, J. *Teaching Social Skills to Children.* Rev. ed.

New York: Pergamon, 1984.

15. Cartledge, G., and Milburn, J., eds. *Teaching Social Skills to Children: Innovative Approaches*. New York: Pergamon, 1980.

16. Centers for Disease Control. *Guidelines for Effective School Health Education to Prevent the Spread of AIDS*. DHHS Publication No. CDC 88–8017. Atlanta: Centers for Disease Control, 1988.

17. Clabby, J. F., and Elias, M. J. *Teach Your Child Decision Making*. New York: Doubleday, 1986.

18. Copple, C.; Siegel, I.; and Saunders, R. *Educating the Young Thinker*. New York: Van Nostrand, 1979.

19. Cornell Cooperative Extension. *Nutrition Education Curriculum*. Ithaca, N.Y.: Cornell Cooperative Extension, 1989.

20. Crabbe, A. "The Future Problem Solving Program." *Educational Leadership* 46 (1989): 27–29.

21. Cuomo, M. *New York State Mentoring Program*. Albany, N.Y.: Governor's School and Business Alliance Task Force, 1989.

22. DeKock, A., and Paul, C. "One District's Commitment to Global Education." *Educational Leadership* 44 (1989): 46–49.

23. DeRisi, W., and Butz, G. *Writing Behavioral Contracts*. Champaign, Ill.: Research Press, 1975.

24. Elias, M. J. "Using Programs for Emotionally Disturbed Children in Mainstreamed or Special Class Settings." In *The Mainstreamed Library: Issues, Ideas, Innovations*, edited by B. Baskin and K. Harris. Chicago: American Library Association, 1982.

25. _____. "Improving Coping Skills of Emotionally Disturbed Boys Through Television-based Social Problem Solving." *American Journal of Orthopsychiatry* 53 (1983): 61–72.

26. _____. *Think Now for Later: Health-Related Stories for Middle School Students*. New Brunswick, N.J.: Rutgers University, 1984.

27. _____. "Schools as a Source of Stress to Children: An Analysis of Causal and Ameliorative Influences." *Journal of School Psychology* 27 (1989): 393–407.

28. _____. "The Role of Affect and Social Relationships in Health Behavior and School Health Curriculum and Instruction." *Journal of School Health* (1990).

29. Elias, M. J., and Branden, L. "Primary Prevention of Behavioral and Emotional Problems in School-Aged Populations." *School Psychology Review* 17 (1988): 581–92.

30. Elias, M. J., and Clabby, J. F. "Integrating Social and Affective Education into Public School Curriculum and Instruction." In *Handbook of Organizational Psychology in the Schools*, edited by C. Maher, R. Illback, and J. Zins, pp. 143–72. Springfield, Ill.: C. C. Thomas, 1984.

31. _____. *Social Decision Making Skills: A Curriculum Guide for the*

Elementary Grades. Rockville, Md.: Aspen, 1989.

32. Elias, M. J.; Gara, M.; and Ubriaco, M. "Sources of Stress and Support in Children's Transition to Middle School: An Empirical Analysis." *Journal of Clinical Child Psychology* 14 (1985): 112–18.

33. Elias, M. J.; Gara, M.; Ubriaco, M.; Rothbaum, P.A.; Clabby, J. F.; and Schuyler, T. "The Impact of a Preventive Social Problem Solving Intervention on Children's Coping with Middle School Stressors." *American Journal of Community Psychology* 14 (1986): 259–75.

34. Elias, M. J., and Maher, C. A. "Social and Affective Development of Children: A Programmatic Perspective." *Exceptional Children* 49 (1983): 339–48.

35. Flaherty, E.; Maracek, J.; Olsen, K.; and Wilcove, G. "Preventing Adolescent Pregnancy: An Interpersonal Problem Solving Approach." *Prevention in Human Services* 2 (1983): 49–64.

36. Freedman, B.; Donahoe, C.; Rosenthal, L.; Schlundt, D.; and McFall, R. "A Social-Behavioral Analysis of Skill Deficits in Delinquent and Nondelinquent Boys." *Journal of Consulting and Clinical Psychology* 46 (1978): 1448–62.

37. Gall, M., and Rhody, T. "Review of Research on Questioning Techniques." In *Questions, Questioning Techniques, and Effective Teaching,* edited by W. Wilen, pp. 23–48. Washington, D.C.: National Education Association, 1987.

38. Garber S., and Associates. *Good Behavior.* New York: Villard Books, 1987.

39. Haboush, K. "An Evaluation of Student Learning Outcomes under a Critical Thinking Social Studies Program." Ph.D. diss., Graduate School of Applied and Professional Psychology, Rutgers University, New Brunswick, N.J., 1988.

40. Halper, A.; Klepp, K.; Murray, D.; Perry, C.; and Smyth, M. *The Minnesota Smoking Prevention Program.* Minneapolis: University of Minnesota School of Public Health, 1986.

41. Huberman, M., and Miles, M. *Innovation Up Close: How School Improvement Works.* New York: Plenum, 1984.

42. Hyman, R. "Discussion Strategies and Tactics." In *Questions, Questioning Techniques, and Effective Teaching,* edited by W. Wilen, 135–52. Washington, D.C.: National Education Association, 1987.

43. Irwin, C. D., Jr. ed. *Adolescent Social Behavior and Health: New Directions for Child Development.* No. 37. San Francisco: Jossey-Bass, 1987.

44. Johnson, D., and Johnson, R. "Social Skills for Successful Group Work." *Educational Leadership* 47, no. 4 (1990): 29–33.

45. Kazdin, A., and Associates. "Problem Solving Skills Training and Relationship Therapy in the Treatment of Antisocial Child Behavior." *Journal of Consulting and Clinical Psychology* 55 (1987): 76–85.

46. King, D. "Broad-Based Support Pushes Health Education Beyond What

the Coach Does Between Sessions." *Association for Supervision and Curriculum Development Update*, June 1986, pp. 1–8.

47. Kniep, W. "Defining a Global Education by Its Content." *Social Education* 50 (1986): 437–45.

48. Kolbe, L. "Why School Health Education? An Empirical Point of View." *Health Education* 16 (1985): 116–20.

49. Lawrence, S. "National Standards and Local Portraits." *Teachers College Record* 91 (1989): 14–17.

50. Levine, D. "Teaching Thinking to At-Risk Students: Generalizations and Speculation." In *At-Risk Students and Thinking: Perspectives from Research*, edited by B. Presseisen, pp. 117–37. Washington, D.C.: National Education Association/Research for Better Schools, 1988.

51. Lipman, M. "Critical Thinking: What Can It be?" *Educational Leadership* 46 (1988): 38–43.

52. London, P. "Character Education and Clinical Intervention: A Paradigm Shift for U.S. Schools." *Phi Delta Kappan* 68 (1987): 667–73.

53. McAuley, R., and McAuley, P. *Child Behavior Problems*. New York: Free Press, 1977.

54. Meier, D. "Comment on the National Standards for American Education Symposium." *Teachers College Record* 91 (1989): 25–27.

55. Mirman, J.; Swartz, R.; and Barell, J. "Strategies to Help Teachers Empower At-Risk Students." In *At-Risk Students and Thinking: Perspectives from Research*, edited by B. Presseisen, pp. 138–56. Washington, D.C.: National Education Association/Research for Better Schools, 1988.

56. National Center for Health Education. *Growing Healthy: Comprehensive School Health Education Program Guide*. New York: American Lung Association, 1985.

57. National Professional School Health Organizations. "Comprehensive School Health Education." *Journal of School Health* 54 (1984): 312–15.

58. Oregon Research Institute. *Project PATH: Programs to Advance Teen Health*. Eugene, Ore.: the Institute, 1986.

59. Patterson, G. *Families: Applications of Social Learning Theory to Family Life*. Champaign, Ill.: Research Press, 1975.

60. Perkins, D. "Thinking Frames." *Educational Leadership* 43 (1986): 4–11.

61. Premack, D. "Reinforcement Theory." In *Nebraska Symposium on Motivation*, edited by D. Levine. Lincoln, Neb.: University of Nebraska Press, 1965.

62. Purdy, C., and Tritsch, L. "Why School Health Education? The Practical Point of View." *Health Education* 16 (1985): 110–12.

63. Raven, J. "Values, Diversity, and Cognitive Development." *Teachers College Record* 89 (1987): 21–38.

64. Reinhartz, J., ed. *Perspectives on Effective Teaching and the Cooperative Classroom*. Washington, D.C.: National Education Association, 1984.

65. Rutter, M. "Psychosocial Resilience and Protective Mechanisms." *American Journal of Orthopsychiatry* 57 (1987): 316–31.
66. Salomon, G. *The Interaction of Media, Cognition and Learning.* San Francisco: Jossey-Bass, 1979.
67. Sarason, S. *The Culture of the School and the Problem of Change.* 2d ed. Boston: Allyn and Bacon, 1982.
68. Slavin, R. *Cooperative Learning: Student Teams.* 2d ed. Washington, D.C.: National Education Association, 1987.
69. _____. *Student Team Learning: An Overview and Practical Guide.* 2d ed. Washington, D.C.: National Education Association, 1988.
70. _____. "Research on Cooperative Learning: Consensus and Controversy." *Educational Leadership* 47, no. 4 (1990): 52–55.
71. Spivack, G.; Platt, J.; and Shure, M. *The Problem Solving Approach to Adjustment.* San Francisco: Jossey-Bass, 1976.
72. Sternberg, R., and Wagner, R., *Practical Intelligence: Nature and Organization or Competence in the Everyday World.* Cambridge: Cambridge University Press, 1986.
73. Wales, C.; Nardi, A.; and Stager, R. "Decision Making: A New Paradigm for Education." *Educational Leadership* 43 (1986): 37–42.
74. Weissberg, R. P. "Designing Effective Social Problem-Solving Problems for the Classroom." In *Peer Relationships and Social Skills in Childhood.* Vol. 2. *Issues in Assessment and Training,* edited by B. Schneider, K. H. Rubin, and J. Ledingham, pp. 225–42. New York: Springer-Verlag, 1985.
75. Whimbey, A. "The Key to Higher-Order Thinking Is Precise Processing." *Educational Leadership* 43 (1984): 66–70.
76. Wilen, W., ed. *Questions, Questioning Techniques, and Effective Teaching.* Washington, D.C.: National Education Association, 1987.
77. Wright, J. C., and Associates. "Perceived TV Reality and Children's Emotional Response." Presentation at the biennial meeting of the Society for Research in Child Development, Kansas City, Mo., April 1989.